THE HERMITAGE

ИВАН ФЕДОРОВ

THE SPATIAL DIMENSIONS OF THE HERMITAGE

MIKHAIL PIOTROVSKY

Director of the State Hermitage

Doctor of History

*Corresponding Member
of the Russian Academy of Sciences*

*Full Member of the Russian Academy
of Arts*

Professor of St Petersburg University

There are few museums in the world of the Hermitage range, and even among them the Hermitage stands out thanks to its exclusive features. Different physical and spiritual spaces cross in the Hermitage, strikingly and sometimes unexpectedly. The metamorphoses occurring with them open up endless images of the artistic universe of the Hermitage. Common notions of dimensions, relationships and movements are not always valid for these spaces. The Hermitage occupies nine buildings today. However, there are more of them in reality. The Winter Palace of Peter the Great, which is situated within the Hermitage Theatre, under its stage, might well be added to them. Another building to be taken into account is the Stock Repository located in the area of Staraya Derevnya, if only half-completed now…

The museum has several symbols. The two principal ones are the Portico with Atlantes at the New Hermitage and the Main Gate of the Winter Palace. The right to typify the Hermitage is challenged by the façades of the museum buildings stretching alongside the Neva. They are marked by a specific architectural and spatial rhythm — majestic and continuous, in contrast with the broken rhythm traceable in the outlines of the islands, the banks of the canals and small rivers of the Neva delta, as well as in the silhouette of the Peter and Paul Fortress on the opposite bank.

During the several recent years Palace Square with the Alexander Column and the Triumphal Arch has also become the Hermitage's emblem of a sort. The handing over to the museum of the eastern wing of the General Staff building has enlarged the direction of the museum's cultural expansion, creating a new vector of movement. The horizontal of the Baroque façades of the Winter Palace and the Classical semicircle of the General Staff make up a dynamic spatial spring. It directs the visitor from the Triumphal Arch across Palace Square, through the Main Gate and the Large Courtyard to the rooms of the Hermitage. It seems to me that this movement symbolizes the incessant advance of the museum itself, constantly changing, overcoming trials and tribulations, but never losing its fundamental traditions. All the wonderful buildings from which the Hermitage consists are not very large. This makes the interiors of the Hermitage palaces even more overwhelming for the visitor. The architecture of the Hermitage buildings itself is one of the museum's highlights — an elegant and edifying "exhibit".

The art book I am introducing by this foreword presents to the reader for the first time a special view of the interior spaces of the Hermitage. The photographers and designers have succeeded in capturing an essential part of the impression evoked by the museum's rooms and halls. The unique spaces of the Hermitage have several dimensions: architectural, artistic, museum proper and historical ones. The walls of the Hermitage remember a great number of crucial events in Russian history. Peter the Great died here, Catherine the Great lived and collected paintings within these walls. Alexander I, the future victor over Napoleon Bonaparte, came to live here after the assassination of his father, Paul I. Nicolas I went to suppress the uprising in December 1825 from this place. He supervised a struggle with a devastating fire in the Winter Palace and created an art museum — the New Hermitage. Stepan Khalturin exploded a bomb under the royal dining-room here, and Tsar-Liberator Alexander II was brought to die here after an explosion of another bomb. Nicholas II opened the first Russian Parliament — the State Duma — in the Winter Palace. The Provisional Government had its sessions in the same palace and was arrested in it after the October Revolution. A peaceful demonstration was shot in front of the Winter Palace in 1905. The palace was assaulted in 1917 by those who got tired of their former life. The Hermitage which witnessed all these historic events, lived through three evacuations — one in connection with Napoleon's invasion in 1812, and two others during the First and Second World Wars. The buildings of the museum saw several revolutions. The Hermitage has become a symbol of the spiritual endurance during the terrible siege in the years of the Second World War, an epitome of beauty resisting evil.

The museum has retained the sense of its name given to it by its founder, Empress Catherine the Great — the Hermitage continues to be a "place of retreat". In any period and under any regimes people come here and find a shelter from everyday problems of the outer world. They remember here about the European component of Russian culture. Its specific feature in general — and in the Hermitage in particular — has always been to bring together diverse artistic traditions that can be traced in the Scythians' golden stags, Matisse's musicians, Buddhist icons and Boucher's *scènes galantes*, in Persian miniatures and Tiepolo's immense canvases. Masterpieces by Rembrandt, Picasso, Canova, Cranach, Giorgione and Monet co-exist within a single space with creations by Friedrich, Leonardo, Raphael, Kandinsky, Poussin and Rubens. They are effectively set out by superb furniture produced by Roentgen and Gambs, gilt bronzes by Thomire, jewellery articles by Pausier and Fabergé, a clock by Cox, porcelain services produced at the Sèvres, Berlin, Vienna and St Petersburg factories. The universe of the Hermitage is illuminated by a whole constellation of brilliant masterpieces of painting, among which the largest stars are glittering — *The Return of the Prodigal Son* by Rembrandt, *Conversation* and *The Dance* by Matisse, *The Nativity of St John the Baptist* by Tintoretto, *St Sebastian* by Titian… The Hermitage collections possess superb examples of small-scale works of art which contribute to the museum's renown no less than its large-scale masterpieces: *The Lady-in-Waiting* and *Perseus and Andromeda* by Rubens, *The Benois Madonna* by Leonardo and *The Madonna Conestabile* by Raphael, *The Luncheon* by Velázquez and genre paintings by the "Small Dutch Masters", the earrings from Theodosia, Limoges enamels, Persian silverware and the ring of Shah Jahan…

The interior spaces in which the Hermitage holdings are displayed, at first sight seem to distract from artistic perception. But that is only at first sight. In actual fact the precious works of art are in harmony with the rooms and halls of the Winter Palace, Small, Old and New Hermitages. They feel themselves especially cosy in the Malachite Drawing-Room and the St George Hall, at the Jordan Staircase, in the Halls of Twelve and Twenty Columns, in the Large Skylight Rooms, the Raphael Loggias, the Alexander Hall and the War Gallery of 1812…

Thus architectural, historical and artistic spaces interact in the Hermitage. Works of art from all times and peoples co-exist in them gladdening any visitor and meeting any taste. You may spend two hours in the Hermitage or you may walk around it with fascination for months. This museum loves its visitors very much.

The priceless collections of the Hermitage, one of the world's most famous museums, are preserved in a beautiful complex of palaces, which is striking for the harmony of its architectural rhythms and its commensurate proportions. Talented architects created, in the course of a century and a half, a group of palaces for the principal imperial residence — the Winter Palace, the buildings of the Small, Large and New Hermitages and the Hermitage Theatre. These buildings serve to this day as a precious setting for the treasures of world art. The place itself where the Hermitage palaces are located in St Petersburg is associated with the most important events in the city's early history. It was here, on the left bank of the Neva, opposite the main fortress, that in November 1705, a little more than two years after the foundation of the northern capital, Peter the Great laid the foundations of the Admiralty, which was to become the major shipyard of new Russia. Soon the first wooden houses of naval officers and shipwrights, Peter's closest associates, began to grow around the Admiralty, primarily upstream the Neva, alongside its low bank. In 1705, on the site of the present-day Palace Embankment with its imposing stone edifices, palaces for the Admiralty com- manders, Russian Vice-Admiral Fiodor Apraxin and Kornelis Kruis, a Norwegian by origin, were built. A little later, in 1708, Peter himself took a decision to move to the left bank of the Neva, closer to the Admiralty, where his first, wooden Winter Palace was under construction. From this time onwards, a rapid transformation of the Neva bank of Admiralty Island, largely due to the Russian monarch's dwelling there, began. In the early 1710s, the first embankment line was made there and the first stone buildings began to appear along it. In 1716–21 the first wooden embankment of the capital was shaped

by adding earth, strengthening and levelling the shoreline between the Admiralty and the Summer Gardens. The cream of young St Petersburg society, inspired by the Emperor's example, started to put up palaces, which were arranged in line as a single façade along the Neva. Besides Peter the Great himself, on the Upper Neva Embankment settled his dignitaries Fiodor Apraxin, Count S. Raguzinsky-Vladislavich, Count Pavel Yaguzhinsky, General Piotr Chernyshov, Admiral Kornelis Kruis, Prince Vasily Dolgoruky and Prince Kantemir. These mansions built according to a single plan by Domenico Trezzini, Jean-Baptiste Le Blond and Georg Johann Mattarnovi, the best architects of St Petersburg in the early

eighteenth century, formed one of the earliest architectural ensembles in St Petersburg. Thus Peter's dream to give the new capital of Russia a European appearance was being realized. After Peter the Great, a succession of empresses and emperors would develop the city and multiply the beauty and glory of the dazzling river façade of St Petersburg. Empress Anna Ioannovna after her return to the city in 1732 immediately settled on the Upper Neva Embankment, in the mansion formerly owned by Fiodor Apraxin. Soon she ordered to erect next to it, near the eastern façade of the Admiralty,

a new building as her Winter Palace, which marked the beginning of the present-day complex of the imperial winter residence. On stretching over the years to the spectacular length of 400 metres, the ensemble engulfed the structures of Peter's age retaining within its thick walls the fragments of the earlier structures. The architectural appearance of the Palace Embankment took its final shape in the reign of Catherine the Great. It was enlarged to the present-day dimensions according to a project by Yury Velten, faced with granite and decorated with expressive descents and bridges making up, together with the palaces of the Hermitage, one of the most remarkable landmarks in St Petersburg.

FOREWORD
by Mikhail Piotrovsky

TEXTS
by Sophia Kudriavtseva (*The Palaces and Interiors*; *Art of European Countries:*
Italy, the Netherlands, France, Spain, Flanders, Holland, England, Germany),
Nina Tarasova (*Art of European Countries: Russia*; *Primitive Art*),
Alexander Butiaghin (*Art of Classical Antiquity*) and Marina Kozlovskaya (*Eastern Art*)

TRANSLATED FROM THE RUSSIAN
by Valery Fateyev

CONCEPT OF THE PROJECT
by Sergei Vesnin

DESIGN AND LAYOUT
by Piotr Kanaikin

PHOTOGRAPHS
by Leonid Bogdanov, Pavel Demidov, Leonard Kheifets, Yury Molodkovets,
Victor Savik, Yevgeny Shliopkin, Yevgeny Siniaver, Vladimir Terebenin,
Oleg Trubsky and Vasily Vorontsov

COLOUR CORRECTION
by Vladimir Glazkov, Vladimir Kniazev, Alexander Kondratov, Liubov Kornilova,
Denis Lazarev and Alexander Miagkov

COMPUTER LAYOUT
by Nina Sokolova

EDITED
by Sergei Vesnin

Work on the edition contributed
by Dmitry Chubarov, Irina Dubrovskaya, Sergei Ludzsky, Maria Lyzhenkova,
Valentina Mikheyeva, Irina Petrova, Dmitry Trofimov and Natalia Zakharova

———————

on p. 4: View of the Winter Palace from the Palace Bridge
on pp. 6 and 7: The Winter Palace. View from Palace Square
on pp. 8 and 9: Panoramic view of the Palace Embankment. Ensemble of the Hermitage buildings

ISBN 5-93893-083-9

THE WINTER PALACE

The priceless collections of the Hermitage, one of the world's greatest museums, are housed in the most splendid palace complex of St Petersburg striking by the harmony of its architectural rhythms and the balance of its proportions. The complex of buildings created by talented architects in the very centre of the Russian capital over a century and a half as the state residence of the Russian Emperors serves now as a precious setting for the artistic treasures preserved in their rooms. The Winter Palace, the buildings of the Small, Old and New Hermitages and the Hermitage Theatre are used now to display the main art exhibitions of the museum. The two separate buildings — the General Staff on Palace Square, once the Ministry of Foreign Affairs and Finance of the Russian Empire, and the palace of Prince Alexander Menshikov, the first governor of St Petersburg, Peter the Great's closest associate — also house the museum's exhibitions now. The unique Hermitage exhibits representing all the facets of world culture from ancient times to the twentieth century perfectly match the magnificent interiors created by celebrated architects and the stories of their provenance are closely related to major events in the history of the Russian capital and the life of the imperial family.

The Palace Bridge across the Neva affords a magnificent view of Palace Square with a panorama of the Hermitage complex. Its most prominent landmark is the Winter Palace built in 1754–62 to a design by Bartolomeo Francesco Rastrelli (1700–1771). The great architect was the son of Bartolomeo Carlo Rastrelli (1675–1744), an Italian sculptor invited to Russia by Peter the Great. The flowering of Rastrelli's genius coincided with the reign of Elizabeth Petrovna, Peter the Great's daughter, who rose to the throne in November 1741 in a palace coup led by the Guards. Empress Elizabeth continued her father's policies aimed at strengthening Russia and heightening its reputation as a mighty autocratic power. The Russian imperial court needed a residence capable to accentuate the enlightened European style of the new Empress.

The first Winter Palace had been put up in St Petersburg earlier, during the reign of Peter the Great. The site on the bank of the Neva, chosen by the founder of the northern capital, was not largely changed during the construction of the later Winter Palaces — the buildings just shifted little by little towards the Admiralty; their dimensions grew and their architectural design became more and more rich and elaborate. On 16 June 1754 Rastrelli's drawings were approved and a special body was formed to oversee the construction. The best masons from different cities of Russia were brought to St Petersburg to build the palace that would become one of the most elegant royal residences in Europe. At last, in the spring of 1761, a new majestic edifice was completed in the centre of St Petersburg. It proved to be a fine example of the Russian Baroque and Rastrelli's most perfect and beautiful creation. Elizabeth Petrovna, however, did not live to move into the newly built residence — she died on 25 December 1761.

1 / 2

THE MAIN (JORDAN) STAIRCASE
→
THE MAIN (JORDAN) STAIRCASE

THE PETER HALL

THE PETER HALL. DETAIL OF VAULT PAINTING

The first owner of the Winter Palace was Elizabeth's nephew, Peter III, who moved to the new imperial residence immediately after a ceremony of its consecration on Easter in 1762. However, it was Catherine II, wife of Peter III, who was destined to become the palace's true owner. She dethroned her husband in June 1762 as a result of a palace coup. This event marked the beginning of the most significant phase in the history of the official imperial residence directly connected with the creation of the Hermitage Museum.

The grand building of the palace, with a large inner courtyard had a majestic look both from the Neva embankment and from the Admiralty. But it was the main façade overlooking Palace Square that produced an especially magnificent impression. The monumental triple arcade,

the dynamic silhouettes of the walls, the virtuoso delineation of the Baroque ornaments and the abundance of moulded decor never ceased to evoke admiration of contemporaries.

Rastrelli's outstanding creation has basically retained its original appearance to this day. An important landmark in the history of the royal palace was a great fire that broke out on 17 December 1837 and practically erased its interiors in two days. The restoration of the palace was carried out in 1837–39 under the supervision of Vasily Stasov (1769–1848) and Alexander Briullov (1798–1877). The present-day Winter Palace is a fanciful combination of various styles and ages blending, however, into a single magnificent whole. Visitors to the museum have a chance to enjoy a rare wealth of architectural fantasies by famous architects. Nowadays, only a few original interiors of the Winter Palace give an idea of the grandeur and scope of Rastrelli's genius. The official part of the palace opens with a majestic JORDAN STAIRCASE. The brilliant architect was at his very best in this interior. The huge space of the staircase sparkling with light opens up suddenly from the austere white-marble arched bays of the ground-floor gallery and the first shaded flight of stairs. Located almost at the height of twenty metres, the ceiling painting that features ancient gods hovering in the sky enhances the illusory effect of infinite space in the Baroque manner. The light pouring from the windows and reflected in the mirrors of the opposite wall, streams along the gilt moulded ornaments and the white marble of the statues of deities and the Muses. Vasily Stasov, who supervised the restoration of this part of the palace, succeeded in retaining Rastrelli's main concept.

The Jordan Staircase of the Winter Palace affords a view of the entrance to the MAIN SUITE — a complex of state rooms intended for official receptions, the so-called "Grandes Entrées" of the imperial family, which were held in connection with major state holidays and church feasts of the Russian Empire. The rooms were destroyed by fire in 1837, but Vasily Stasov partly recreated their former majestic appearance during his restoration. The architectural, pictorial and sculptural decor of the Main Suite was shaped strictly in keeping with a definite programme. Its main goal was to create within the imperial residence the Pantheon of Russian martial glory, a memorial complex designed to celebrate the outstanding events of Russian history and their participants.

The FIELD MARSHAL HALL, created in 1833–34 by Auguste de Montferrand, was embellished with portraits of the most prominent Russian military figures: Count Piotr Rumiantsev-Zadunaisky, Prince Grigory Potemkin-Tavrichesky, Count Alexander Suvorov-Rymniksky, Prince Mikhail Kutuzov-Smolensky, Count Ivan Diebitsch-Zabalkansky and Count Ivan Paskevich-Erivansky. The large-scale portrait of the latter by Franz von Krüger can now be seen again in the decor of the Field Marshal Hall. This austere white-marble hall had an ill repute — it was here that the fire, which destroyed the entire Winter Palace within thirty hours, began on 17 December 1837. The doors lead from this hall to the next interiors of the Main Suite that have also retained their memorial significance.

The PETER HALL (or the SMALL THRONE ROOM) was devoted to the memory of Peter the Great, the founder of the Russian Empire. The hall was designed by Auguste de Montferrand in 1833 and restored after the fire by Vasily Stasov

almost without any alterations. All the details of the architectural decor were connected with the name of the great Russian reformer. In the centre of the hall, in a semicircular niche, is an allegorical canvas, *Peter the Great with the Goddess of Wisdom Minerva* by Jacopo Amiconi. Near it, on a special dais, stands the Tsar's throne commissioned by Empress Anna Ioannovna from the English master craftsman Nicholas Clausen in 1731. The walls of the room are lined with red Lyons velvet embroidered with a silver ornament. Interwoven into the ornament are the repeatedly used elements of the imperial attributes: the monogram of Peter the Great, the Tsar's crown and the state emblem in the shape of double-headed eagle. Imperial symbolism included into the ornamental design of the ceiling and the painted decorative panels featuring the famous battles of the Northern War — the Battle of Poltava and the Battle of Lesnaya — promoted the perception of this interior as the "palladium of Russian grandeur and glory".

Each of the subsequent rooms of the suite develops the theme of the celebration of the Fatherland. The ARMORIAL HALL created by Vasily Stasov as an exemplar of a Classical hall with columns, belonged to the group of the Winter Palace's formal reception rooms and served as an introductory interior to the Large Throne Room. In the late eighteenth century this place, decorated to a design by Yury Velten, became known as the White Gallery. In the reign of Catherine the Great sumptuous balls were held here. In 1796 Emperor Paul I had the Mourning Hall arranged in this interior for the ceremony of leave-taking. It was remarkable that the ceremony was devoted to the memory of both Catherine the Great who had just died and her consort Peter III killed in 1762 after his wife's coup. A huge catafalque shaped like a rotunda with a lifted dome was placed in the middle of the hall. The lifted dome contained two coffins with the remains of the Russian Sovereigns, the consorts who had become enemies in their struggle for the throne. In the first quarter of the nineteenth century the White Gallery began to be used again according to its original designation. It was again the venue for noisy masquerades, majestic receptions and balls. Nicholas I, however, decided to use it for different aims. The new architectural and artistic image of this room was based on the glorification of the state system of the Russian Empire. Near the side walls were placed sculptural groups of ancient Russian knights, made of papier-mâché, holding standards to which coloured signs with emblems of the Russian provinces were attached. The same heraldic motif was included into the decor of huge bronze chandeliers. They are adorned with the coats-of-arms of Russian cities to this day. This vast interior vividly contrasts with the adjacent Peter Hall not only by its dimensions, but also by its bright colour scheme, unusually vivid for Classicism. The striking colour range of the hall is based on the violent contrast of snow-white decor of the walls and the glistening gold of the Corinthian colonnades, cornice, balustrade and the upper tier of windows. The stately image of the

5

VIEW OF THE ARMORIAL HALL

Armorial Hall is emphasized by the majestic rhythm of its French windows alternating with the massive columns gilded from top to bottom. Facing the Large Courtyard of the Winter Palace, they are vividly reflected in the mirrored windows of the opposite wall of the

6 / 7 / 8

THE ARMORIAL HALL.
VIEW OF THE WESTERN WALL

THE ARMORIAL HALL

THE ARMORIAL HALL. DETAIL OF THE INTERIOR

gallery that served as a pathetic introduction to the Large Throne Room or St George Hall. Between the two main formal interiors — the Armorial Hall and the Large Throne Room — lies the most famous memorial room of the palace — the 1812 War Gallery dedicated to the victory of the Russian Army over Napoleon Bonaparte. The gallery was designed by Carlo Rossi (1775/77–1849) and the ceremony of its opening was held on 25 December 1826, the anniversary of Napoleon's expulsion from Russia. The ceremony was attended by the imperial court, generals, officers and soldiers awarded for their participation in the "Patriotic War" of 1812 and the Russian armies' foreign campaign of 1813–14. It was the first time that a gallery at the heart of the imperial residence, near the Large Throne Room, was adorned with portraits of true combat heroes rather than the crowned owners of the palace. 332 portraits of partic-ipants in the War of 1812 were placed there — the war generals or those who received a general's rank right after the end of the war. This memorial structure was modelled on a hall in Windsor Castle that was devoted to the memory of the Waterloo Battle and

9 / 10

THE 1812 WAR GALLERY

FRANZ VON KRÜGER. 1797–1857
EQUESTRIAN PORTRAIT OF ALEXANDER I. 1837
Oil on canvas. 484 x 344 cm

accommodated the portraits of the heads of state and military leaders of the Belle Alliance painted by Thomas Lawrence. The portraits in the War Gallery of the Winter Palace were painted in the studio of George Dawe, an English painter invited by Alexander I to carry out this large commission in Russia. Dawe worked on the imperial commission with two assistants, Wilhelm Golike and Alexander Poliakov. The Gallery also housed large-scale formal portraits of the European monarchs — the Russian Emperor Alexander I, Frederick William III of Prussia and Franz Joseph I, Emperor of Austria — the allies of Russia in the anti-Napoleonic coalition. Portraits of military leaders — the Duke of Wellington, who received the title of the Russian Field Marshal for the victory in the Battle of Waterloo, the Field Marshals Mikhail Barclay de Tolly, Mikhail Kutuzov and Grand Duke Konstantin Pavlovich — could be also seen there. Moreover, for the first time in the history of the imperial residence the gallery was adorned with portraits of the rankers from the Company of the Palace Grenadiers who rescued all the canvases during the fire of 1837 (the portraits were returned to the their original places after Stasov's restoration of the hall). A distinctive feature of the 1812 War Gallery is a striking integrity of its interior in which the portraits of national heroes are perfectly blended with its decor creating a harmonious image of a veritable architectural and artistic ensemble.

The 1812 War Gallery opens up the space of the ST GEORGE HALL (the LARGE THRONE ROOM), an architectural and thematic culmination of the Main Suite. Catherine the Great commissioned the architect Giacomo Quarenghi (1744–1817) to design a new throne room instead of Rastrelli's outfashioned Baroque hall which no longer satisfied the rational spirit of the Enlightenment. Created in 1787–95, the interior was resolved in austere Classical forms. However, Quarenghi's recognized masterpiece, a splendid monumental hall with

two tiers of windows adorned with double columns of natural coloured marble, perished during the fire. Vasily Stasov preserved only the general proportions and architectural articulations of the interior. Emperor Nicholas I ordered to make "the entire St George Hall in white marble". The walls and columns were faced by expensive white Carrara marble with bluish streaks, a variety brought in the form of slabs and even whole columns from Italy. The favourite material of Italian sculptors, sparkling with thousands of shades, enhanced the varicoloured palette of the inlaid parquet floor made up of sixteen different kinds of wood. The gilt pattern embossed in the copper of the suspended metal ceiling repeated the floor ornament in a mirror-like manner. The marble bas-relief with a representation of the victorious St George by the Italian master Francesco del Nero was placed above the Throne. Owing to the difficulties related to the delivery from Italy and the mounting of fragile marble details, the St George Hall was consecrated later than other rooms in the palace — in 1841. In this hall manifestos

21 / **22**

THE ST GEORGE HALL. THE THRONE

THE ST GEORGE HALL

24

declaring wars and concluding peace, introducing changes in the state system of the Empire and other reforms were read. One of the most memorable events was the ceremony of the establishment of the first Russian parliament, the State Duma, in 1906. After the revolution of 1917 the St George Hall lost the most important element of its architectural decoration — the monumental Throne that completed the perspective of the principal formal interior of the Winter Palace. In December 2000 the Throne was recreated by the efforts of Hermitage restorers.

The Large Throne Room and the nearby Large Church complete the Main Staircase of the Winter Palace. It was to this place that the court festive processions, the *Grandes Entrées* of the imperial family, were marching, to be concluded with church services. Created to a design by Rastrelli, the Large Church was consecrated in 1762 to the Resurrection of Christ. However, a year later the icon of the Vernicle was brought to the church and it was consecrated again to the Saviour

23 / 24

THE HALL OF FRENCH ROCOCO ART

THE DOME OF THE GREAT CHURCH

25 / 26

THE GOLDEN DRAWING-ROOM

THE BOUDOIR

of the Vernicle. In 1807 the Large Church of the Winter Palace received the status of cathedral. The original decor of the church interior, devastated by the fire of 1837, was reconstructed to a design by Vasily Stasov. The architect, who aimed at recreating Rastrelli's design as exactly as possible, restored the iconostasis and elements of the painted and architectural decoration. A large part of the church decoration was executed in papier-mâché to replace labour-consuming process of wood-carving. The Russian painters Fiodor Bruni and Piotr Basin decorated the pendentives and ceiling of the church parvis. The interior of the Large Church suffered a great damage again in the 1940s when the iconostasis carved by P. Kretan was demolished. Some surviving elements of the iconostasis have enabled restorers to work out a convincing project of its restoration.

A small passage links the official and living sections of the Winter Palace located in the part of the building facing Palace Square. In the reign of Catherine the Great this part of the palace was employed as her private apartments. In the 1830s and 1840s, a larger part of rooms in the south block of the building was decorated to designs by Alexander Briullov. Especially remarkable among them is the Alexander Hall dedicated to the memory of Emperor

Alexander I, as well as the suite of five state rooms which were used to display large paintings illustrating the heroic episodes of Russian war history. Now they house one of the best collections of the Hermitage including masterpieces of eighteenth-century French art.

Of particular historical, architectural and artistic value are the rooms of the so-called First Reserve Section of the Winter Palace, formerly the private apartments inhabited by the owners of the imperial residence. Especially remarkable for luxury and brilliance were the interiors decorated for the wedding of the heir to the throne, the future Emperor Alexander II. Work on these interiors began at the same time as the restoration of the Winter Palace after the fire and was completed by April 1841. The main interior of the so-called New Apartments of the heir was the White Hall lit by two tiers of windows. The adjoining group of apartments belonged to his consort, Maria Alexandrovna. The neighbouring GOLDEN DRAWING-ROOM, designed by Alexander Briullov for the grand duchess, the future Empress, deserves particular attention. Originally its walls and vault were covered with a white artificial marble and gilding was used only to highlight the thin molded ornament. In the 1860s and 1870s the walls of the hall were gilded all over under the supervision of Vladimir Schreiber. It was in this room that during the tragic days for Russia, after the assassination of Alexander II by terrorists on 1 March 1881, the new Russian Emperor Alexander III discussed with some members of the State Council the future of Russia. He was to decide the destiny of the Russian Constitution and Reforms, which had become his father's life work and which he had failed to complete. Next to the Golden Drawing-Room are the private apartments of Empress Maria Alexandrovna. The BOUDOIR is the most prominent among them for its elegance and splendour. The interior was completely redesigned in 1853 by Harald Bosse (1812–1894) in keeping with the demands of a new fashion. Similarly to an elegant snuff-box, this small room is stylized in the spirit

29

of Rococo with an abundance of carved and gilt ornaments, mirrors and painted insets. A step and a low railing separate a part of the Boudoir shaped like an alcove. The cloth of pomegranate shade for the wall panels, furniture upholstery, draperies on the windows, and doors was commissioned in France at the Cortier Factory. One of the most impressive interiors designed by Briullov in the Winter Palace is the MALACHITE DRAWING-ROOM, formerly a private apartment of Nicholas I's wife, Empress Alexandra Fiodorovna. At the Emperor's desire, Briullov amply used in the decor of this room a rare semiprecious stone — malachite. This strikingly beautiful green stone began to be more widely used in the 1830s, after huge deposits of malachite had been discovered at the Demidovs' mines in the Urals. Malachite was employed in the Empress's drawing-room to face the columns, pilasters and fireplace, by means of the complex and laborious technique known as "Russian mosaic". Thin layers of malachite were pasted on to the base and the joints were filled with malachite powder, then the surface was polished. The combination of malachite with rich gilding of the vault, doors, capitals of the columns and pilasters produced a striking effect. Guests did not know what to amaze at — "the luxury of the material or the luxury of the artist's work in this temple of wealth and taste". The room was set with furniture

27 / 28

THE MALACHITE DRAWING-ROOM

DETAIL OF A FIREPLACE FROM THE MALACHITE DRAWING-ROOM

executed in 1830 by the cabinet-maker Heinrich Gambs after drawings by Auguste de Montferrand and saved during the fire. The Malachite Drawing-Room leads to the majestic halls of the Neva Suite and the Main (Jordan) Staircase which complete the precious necklace of the historical interiors of the Winter Palace. Located along the northern façade of the Winter Palace, they were conceived for official ceremonies. Originally the enfilade of rooms running from the State Staircase alongside the Neva ended with the Throne Room striking by its Baroque opulence. In the late eighteenth century Giacomo Quarenghi, court architect to Catherine the Great, created instead of the five rooms of the Neva Suite three new interiors — the Fore Hall, the Great Fore Hall, or Nicholas Hall, and the Concert Hall. In the decor of these formal halls, an elegant restraint of Classicism ousted the unbridled Baroque fantasies with light and colour. The architect Vasily Stasov, who restored the Neva Suite after the fire of 1837, left Quarenghi's design largely unaltered. However, he made the halls even more grand and monumental — the white marble of the walls and columns further enhanced the immense space of the interior and filled it with air.

The focal point of the suite is the NICHOLAS or LARGE HALL, the largest state room of the Winter Palace (it is 1,103 sq. metres in area). The purpose of the CONCERT HALL adjoining it could be easily guessed from its decor — its second tier had statues of the Muses and classical deities by the sculptor Johann Hermann, while the decorative grisaille painting of the cove linking the ceiling and the walls included allegorical figures with the attributes of the arts. The Concert Hall displays the Hermitage collection of Russian silverware from the seventeenth to the early twentieth century, with a unique eighteenth-century memorial ensemble, the silver shrine of St Alexander Nevsky, as its centrepiece.

29

THE CONCERT HALL

THE SMALL HERMITAGE

The building of the Small Hermitage — the next edifice after the Winter Palace in the line of buildings running along the Palace Embankment — was created by the two gifted architects, Jean-Baptiste Vallin de la Mothe (1729–1800) and Yury Velten (1730–1801). They realized Catherine's wish to have one more, little palace next to the imperial residence. Such buildings which became fashionable in the early eighteenth century were usually put up amidst a calm garden or park and were intended for pastimes in the circle of choice guests. Such pavilions were usually called *hermitages* in the French manner, the word meaning an abode of a recluse or a retired place. Catherine the Great used her "Hermitage" in the centre of St Petersburg as a place where she could relax from the strict routine of ceremonial court life established in the Winter Palace. She liked to spend her leisure there in a friendly company forgetting about affairs of state. Catherine surrounded herself in the Hermitage with fine works of art and precious articles. Thus the Empress's whim laid the foundation for the new complex of buildings which were used not only for gatherings of the narrow circle of the Empress's friends, lovers of exquisite pastimes, but as an accommodation for the imperial collections of world art. Gradually Catherine's Hermitage grew into a world-famous museum bequeathed by the great Empress to posterity.

It began with the Hanging Garden (*Hortus pencilis*), raised on high vaults to the first-floor level of the Winter Palace. Here trees were planted in tubs covered outside with lead and filled with earth, and flowerbeds were laid out. The paths were lined with white marble statues. The architectural project of the garden owes much to Vallin de la Mothe, while Yury Velten was responsible for its construction in 1764–75. Simultaneously with the creation of the "upper garden" the architect erected in its southern part about 1766 the Pavilion for the Empress's favourite Count Grigory Orlov and linked it by a passageway with Catherine's private apartments in the Winter Palace opposite it. Later it came to be called the Southern Pavilion of the Small Hermitage. At the end of the eighteenth century the pavilion was a dwelling place of the Empress's favourites and later of members of the imperial family and major court dignitaries.

On completing the Southern Pavilion, the architect Velten erected the Northern or Orangery Pavilion at the opposite end of the Hanging Garden after a design by Vallin de la Mothe in 1769. Here, at the level of the first floor, were the Orangery, the Toplight Hall, five studies and the *hermitage* proper. This was a room where "small hermitages" or entertaining parties, during which the hostess was on equal terms with her guests, took place. Catherine the Great was fond of these private soirées during which dinners were followed by reading, conversations, performances and games. From that period onwards the palace was called the Hermitage. (The present-day name, the Small Hermitage, became associated with this edifice only in the middle of the nineteenth century, after the construction nearby of the Old and New Hermitage buildings, when these two palaces, forming

30 / 31 / 32 / 33 / 34

THE WINTER PALACE AND THE NORTHERN PAVILION OF THE SMALL HERMITAGE

VIEW OF MILLIONNAYA STREET FROM THE WINDOWS OF THE WINTER PALACE
→

THE *PEACOCK* CLOCK. Second half of the 18th century England. By James Cox

THE PAVILION HALL

THE PAVILION HALL. ARCADE

a unified architectural complex, began to be called by the general name of the Large Hermitage.) However, the Empress conceived to use the new palace not for amusements alone, but also as the Museum of Imperial Art Collections which she had begun to assemble intensely from the first years of her reign. It was for them, and primarily for the first collection of paintings acquired by Catherine from the Berlin merchant Johann Ernest Gotzkowsky in 1764, that Velten put up two picture galleries along the eastern and western borders of the Hanging Garden.

The overall layout of Catherine's Hermitage, picture galleries, Hanging Garden and pavilions was basically preserved intact until the middle of the nineteenth century. It was partly retained after the reconstruction of the building by the architect Vasily Stasov in the early 1840s, too. The Eastern Gallery was used in the middle of the nineteenth century to house two displays. One of them, the Gallery of Jewellery of the Imperial Court, contained the collections of jewels and other valuable items now preserved in the Hermitage's Gold Room. The Gallery of Peter the Great housed Peter's personal belongings kept after his death in the Kunstkammer (Cabinet of Curios) and transferred to the Hermitage in 1848. In 1850-58 the interiors of the Northern Pavilion were redecorated. Instead of Catherine's premises, Andrei Stakenschneider (1802–1865) created there the magnificent Pavilion Hall faced with white marble. Its elegant decor combined

40

the Renaissance motifs with exquisite details of Moorish architecture. The openwork arcades, two-tiered colonnades of white Carrara marble, reliefs, gilt stucco mouldings, elegant railings of the upper galleries and a unique copy of an ancient mosaic ceiling, all adds to the beauty of this interior. On the side of the Hanging Garden Stakenschneider attached to the Pavilion Hall the Winter Garden and covered it with a glazed tent-shaped ceiling. In the centre, amidst evergreen exotic plants, he installed a marble fountain executed by the Italian sculptor Felice de Fovo. In 1939 the romantic Winter Garden was demolished, but the fountain has remained at the same place in the Hanging Garden. Nowadays the hall houses a collection of so-called mosaic tables from the eighteenth and nineteenth centuries. Their unique table-tops are adorned with fine mosaic patterns in the Florentine and Roman techniques. But the focus of attention in this magnificent display is the famous Peacock Clock created in the eighteenth century by the English master craftsman James Cox. The clock was acquired by Prince Grigory Potemkin and brought to St Petersburg in a dismantled state. Only in 1792 the famous Russian craftsman Ivan Kulibin succeeded to assemble and set the sophisticated mechanism in motion. The clock was kept in the Tauride Palace. After Potemkin's death it became part of the collection of Catherine the Great and occupied the pride of place in the Eastern Gallery of the Small Hermitage.

35 / 36 / 37

THE SMALL HERMITAGE
THE HANGING GARDEN. THE CENTRAL PATH

THE SMALL HERMITAGE
THE HANGING GARDEN. FOUNTAIN. Mid-19th century
Sculptor Felice de Fovo

THE PAVILION HALL
DETAIL OF A TABLE WITH THE MOSAIC *A DAY IN ROME.*
Mid-19th century. Italy

THE OLD HERMITAGE
THE HERMITAGE THEATRE

The Old or Large Hermitage was built to a design by Yuri Velten in 1770–87 for the rapidly growing collections of Catherine the Great because of cramped condition in the Small Hermitage. Originally the second Hermitage structure put up alongside the Palace Embankment, was called "the structure in line with the Hermitage" and changed its name only in the middle of the nineteenth century, when the Imperial Museum was attached to it. It was then that the building "in line with the Hermitage" began to be named the Old Hermitage and the edifice erected on the side of Large Millionnaya Street, the New Hermitage. So the architectural history of the building turned out to be closely interwoven with the development of the entire complex of the imperial residence. It can be divided into two periods. The first one encompasses the late eighteenth and early twentieth centuries when the building "in line with the Hermitage" was formed as an independent structure. The second period is connected with a radical reconstruction of the Old Hermitage in the middle of the nineteenth century when the interior design of the building was changed.

The construction of the Old Hermitage in the eighteenth century was carried out in two phases. At first Velten erected a small block linking it by a passage with the Small Hermitage. Then Catherine the Great ordered him to enlarge it to the corner of the Palace Embankment and the Winter Canal. Soon after putting up the Hermitage Theatre on the opposite bank of the canal, Velten spanned the Winter Canal with an arched passageway thus linking the whole architectural ensemble of the imperial residence facing the Neva. The architect paid a special attention to the decor of the first-floor interiors of the Old Hermitage that formed together the Neva Suite. The Empress passed this suite during her official *Grandes Entrées* after performances in the Hermitage Theatre. The ceremony of passing through the rooms adorned with paintings of the Italian, Spanish and Dutch schools, glyptic and numismatic collections usually ended in the Northern Pavilion of the Small Hermitage by a large assembly, or *hermitage*, attended by up to 300 guests.

In the early 1850s, in connection with the construction of a special museum building, the New Hermitage, and the transfer to it of a larger part of the collections, the designation and decor of the interiors of the Old Hermitage were altered. Since the lower storeys of the building were to accommodate the State Council and the Cabinet of Ministers of the Russian Empire, the architect Andrei Stakenschneider created on the place of the Oval Hall, where Voltaire's library had been kept in Catherine's reign, the State Staircase linking the rooms of the State Council with the Small Hermitage and the Winter Palace. The elegant white marble staircase, known also as the Council Staircase, leads to the landing of the first floor skirted with slender columns of white Carrara marble. The ceiling painted by the French eighteenth-century artist

THE HERMITAGE THEATRE

VIEW OF THE OLD HERMITAGE FROM THE NEVA

43

Gabriel François Doyen is the only part of decor retained by Stakenschneider from the Oval Hall. The painting shows *Virtues Introducing Young Russians to Minerva*, an allegory reminding that the Hermitage had once belonged to the "Russian Minerva", as Catherine the Great, a patroness of sciences, arts and crafts, was sometimes called. Stakenschneider left the layout of the rooms beginning from the Council Staircase unaltered, although he redecorated them in the historiate style. An architect with a subtle taste and creative imagination, he achieved consummate perfection combining elements of diverse historical styles and a variety of art forms and materials.

The room following the Council Staircase housed in the 1840s one of the best collections of the Imperial Hermitage — paintings by the great Dutch artist Rembrandt. After the construction of the New Hermitage had been completed and the collections of painting moved there, Stakenschneider radically changed the designation and decor of the interior. He filled the space of the Reception Room that was arranged there with abundant decorative details, coloured or glistening with gold: the eight columns of green Revnevaya jasper with gilt capitals set along the walls, rested upon the pedestals of grey and red artificial marble. Fireplaces decorated with coloured marble and gilding were installed at the ends of the hall instead of the former Swedish stoves. Decorative pilasters with painted panels adorned the snow-white artificial marble walls. Thus a museum interior was converted into a stately reception room. Today it is used to display a collection of early Italian painting or the Proto-Renaissance. In the late nineteenth and early twentieth centuries such works were called "primitives", hence the name of the room — the Room of Italian Primitives.

The Large Toplight Hall of the Old Hermitage in the late eighteenth and early nineteenth centuries housed the collection of Italian painters of the fifteenth to early nineteenth centuries and was known as the Italian Hall. Its decor was simple and austere. Stakenschneider transformed the hall into a luxurious palatial interior striking by a variety of its decor in rare materials. Of especial beauty are the red-green columns of band jasper set on fireplaces of white Carrara marble. The fireplaces are embellished with lapis lazuli and mosaic panels. The unique doors of the hall executed of ebony are decorated with an ornament imitating the Boulle technique — a combination of tortoise-shell and gilt copper. The painted panels by Alessandro Padovanino (Varotari) had been in this interior before the reconstruction. Stakenschneider added to them several smaller panels by Fiodor Bruni. Over the doors are medallions with the portraits of Field Marshals Rumiantsev, Suvorov, Kutuzov and Paskevich. Nowadays two masterpieces, *The Benois Madonna* and *The Litta Madonna* by Leonardo da Vinci, are displayed in this magnificent room and that is why it is named after this great Italian artist.

Towards the end of the 1850s the decoration of the new halls and rooms of the New Hermitage was completed. These living apartments were intended for the son of Emperor Alexander II's son, the Heir Tsesarevich Nikolai Alexandrovich. But the heir died at Nice in 1865 and his rooms, which he had never seen, became one of the palace's reserve sections. In the second half of the nineteenth century and in the early twentieth the rooms of the state suite were used for different purposes. Until 1899 they had housed a vast collection of the French and Flemish schools of painting, which were transferred to the rooms of the New Hermitage (after the works of the Russian school were handed over to the newly established Russian Museum of Alexander III). So the suite rooms again became living apartments of the so-called 7th Reserve Section of the Winter Palace. Sometimes the luxurious apartments were put at the disposal of the noted guests of the imperial court. Several decades later the rooms were given back to the museum. Now these architectural settings of the mid-nineteenth century are used to display

THE COUNCIL STAIRCASE
→
THE LEONARDO DA VINCI ROOM

one of the most celebrated Hermitage's collections — Italian art of the Renaissance. The building of the Old Hermitage occupies a place on the Palace Embankment limited from the east by the narrow Winter Canal linking the two rivers — the wide, deep Neva and the small, winding Moika. On the opposite bank of the Winter Canal once stood the Winter Palace of Peter the Great built during his reign, but towards the end of the eighteenth century it became dilapidated and deserted. In 1783 Catherine the Great ordered Giacomo Quarenghi, her court architect, to erect a new court theatre there. A decree about its construction was signed on 6 November 1783. And two years later, on 16 November 1785, a record was made in the court journal informing that the Empress, together with her most august family, "...proceeded through the Hermitage to the new theatre and attended a rehearsal of a comic opera." Quarenghi succeeded in creating a veritable masterpiece — one of the most perfect palatial theatres in Russia and Europe. The architect used the ground floor of the former Winter Palace of Peter the Great as a basement and put up on it a majestic auditorium and a stage. The theatre begins with a foyer located in the upper part of the arched bridge. The two longitudinal walls of the hall, pierced with windows from top to bottom, create an illusion of an open space over the expanses of the Neva on the one side and over the closed elegant world of the St Petersburg palaces running along the Moika on the other. The foyer has acquired its present-day appearance in 1904, after a new redecoration, undertaken by the architect Leonty Benois in imitation of the Rococo style. The auditorium is remarkable for its balanced proportions. Taking the form of the ancient Roman theatre as his model, Quarenghi resolved the rows in the shape of an amphitheatre. The architect described the specific features of the Hermitage Theatre designed by him as follows: "In this theatre, free of any formal etiquette, there are no special seats and anyone may seat anywhere he or she likes." Quarenghi adorned the scenic portal and the walls with Corinthian semi-columns and niches and faced them with polychrome artificial marble. He skilfully introduced into the ensemble of the auditorium decorative reliefs and pieces of sculpture featuring the heavenly and earthly gods of the theatre. The architect himself wrote about his work: "...in the ten niches of the auditorium and proscenium I set up the statues of Apollo and the Nine Muses, while in the squares over the niches I installed the busts — medallions of contemporary theatrical celebrities, namely the two most famous composers, Jommelli and Buranello, and the poets Metastasio, Molière, Racine, Voltaire, Sumarokov and others." The theatre skilfully designed by Giacomo Quarenghi became the favourite resting place of Empress Catherine the Great. It harmoniously combined the best accomplishments of European theatrical architecture — excellent acoustics, comfortable stage, cosy seats for spectators — with an elegance and a sense of intimacy befitting a domestic imperial theatre. Usually the entire royal court, the heir's family and diplomats were present at performances — up to 200 invited persons. The architecture of the auditorium delighted contemporaries and confirmed the designer's opinion that the shape of covered amphitheatre was the most comfortable one. As he said, spectators "see each other well and when the auditorium is full of people, it is a pleasant sight". The Empress had an eye on the staging of productions and herself indulged in play-writing. The Hermitage Theatre staged operas, comedies and dramas. Among the theatre's conductors were such European celebrities as Cimarosa, Galuppi and Paisiello. The traditions of the Hermitage Theatre have been recently revived. Today plays are shown on its stage and well-known artists from leading St Petersburg, Russian and world companies perform in it again.

A remarkable feature of the Hermitage Theatre is the memorial exhibition "The Winter Palace of Peter the Great" arranged on its ground floor. It has been created in the building quite recently. A research in the basements of the Hermitage Theatre undertaken in the course of its restoration carried out in 1987–89 by the Hermitage specialists revealed authentic architectural fragments of the former Peter's palace. The construction of the Winter Palace of Peter the Great began in 1716 according to a design by Georg Johann Mattarnovi and was completed in 1723, shortly before Peter's death, by Domenico Trezzini. Since Giacomo Quarenghi did not destroy the original building using the ground floor of the palace of Peter the Great as the foundation of the Hermitage Theatre, it became possible to recreate, two hundred years later, a section of his inner courtyard, a gallery with an arcade and a part of the interiors.

42 / 43

THE STATE SUITE OF THE OLD HERMITAGE

THE PROTO-RENAISSANCE ROOM

The rooms of the third and last Winter Palace of Peter the Great survived without any decoration. The reconstructed interiors of the Dining-Room, Study and Turnery display objects used at the royal court during the early phase of the northern Russian capital and later kept in the Hermitage reserves. In the courtyard, surviving in a very good state, with the pavement of the Petrine age, stands a carriage made shortly before Peter's death after drawings by Nicholas Pineau.

Now the exhibition of the Palace of Peter the Great includes the posthumous wax effigy of the Tsar produced by Bartolomeo Carlo Rastrelli. Plaster casts from Peter's face, hands and feet were made by the sculptor soon after the Emperor's death. The completed work was an exact copy of his outward appearance. All his clothes — the festive costume embroidered in silver, the Order of St Andrew the First-Called with a red order ribbon, shoes and even a wig — are authentic. Thus two historical ages covered with the glory of the two great emperors, Peter I and Catherine II, have met in the Hermitage Theatre.

44 / 45

THE HERMITAGE THEATRE. THE AUDITORIUM

THE ARCHED PASSAGEWAY OF THE HERMITAGE THEATRE OVER THE WINTER CANAL

THE NEW HERMITAGE

The idea to build the New Hermitage, a museum that would gather within its walls the artistic treasures of the imperial family previously dispersed in the collections of the Small and Old Hermitage, in the Tauride and Anichkov Palaces, at Tsarskoye Selo and Peterhof and in other royal palaces, belonged to Nicholas I. It was on his orders that in 1842–51 the area near the Winter Palace was used for the construction of a new museum that completed the architectural complex of the St Petersburg imperial residence. The Russian emperor entrusted the project to Leo von Klenze (1784–1864), the Bavarian architect responsible for the two famous museums, the Pinakothek and the Glyptothek in Munich, built to accommodate paintings and sculptures of King Ludwig I. Nicholas I attended the Munich museums in 1838 and, greatly impressed by them, commissioned Leo von Klenze to design the "Imperial Museum" in St Petersburg. The task set by the Russian monarch surpassed in scale and complexity all the architect's previous projects. He was to embody in the New Hermitage, practically the first art museum in Russia, the most progressive ideas of a Museum as a universal repository of the artistic experience of mankind. The huge imperial collections were to be arranged in it according to a clear-cut system allowing visitors to get the fullest possible notion of the history of world art. Moreover, Nicholas I made an express demand that the façades and interiors of the Imperial Museum should have a luxurious appearance befitting the status of an imperial residence. So Klenze designed the New Imperial Hermitage as a museum within the museum. His building harmoniously blended various forms and genres of the fine arts and architecture. The exterior of the majestic palace designed in a neo-Greek style was adorned with an impressive architectural symbol — a portico with ten atlantes. Carved of Serdobol granite in the studio of the Russian sculptor Alexander Terebenev, the protico with the mighty figures supporting it serves, like the ancient Propylaea, as an entrance to the Temple of High Art. Apart from Klenze, an important role in the creation of the New Hermitage belonged to the Building Commission that included the leading architects and engineers of St Petersburg. Two of its members, the architects Vasily Stasov and Nikolai Yefimov, were in fact the designer's co-authors as they carried out the project of Leo von Klenze and made some amendments in it. However, the unique decor of each room, gallery and study of the New Hermitage followed Klenze's plans and therefore it is mainly to the German architect that we owe the fascinating sense of integrity characteristic of the building, despite all the wealth and variety of its decor. According to the general plan, the rooms of the ground floor of the New Hermitage were given for the collections of sculpture, while the rooms of the upper floor were to accommodate the collections of paintings of the imperial museum. The three Large Skylight Halls made up the main suite on the first floor of the building. They owed their names to the unique

46 / 47 / 48

THE NEW HERMITAGE. PORTICO WITH ATLANTES

VIEW OF THE NEW HERMITAGE
FROM THE WINTER CANAL
→
THE LARGE ITALIAN SKYLIGHT HALL

type of giant vaulted ceilings crowned with glazed lanterns through which light streamed into the halls. It was in these interiors that the largest paintings of the Italian and Spanish schools, for which daylight was thought to be most favourable, were hung. The noble shining of gilt mouldings of the vaults and the painted dark red walls provided a fine setting for a majestic display which perfectly united masterpieces by the Great Masters, luxurious tables, vases, lamp stands and other decorative objects of malachite, porphyry, rhodonite, jasper and lapis lazuli made at the Peterhof, Yekaterinburg and Kolyvan Lapidary Works. On the side of the Winter

Canal the Large Skylight Halls adjoin a long gallery which is a replica of Raphael's Loggias in the Vatican. Built in the sixteenth century by the celebrated architect Bramante and decorated with frescoes by Raphael and his pupils, it was reproduced in St Petersburg at the behest of Catherine the Great in 1783–92. Giacomo Quarenghi made all necessary architectural measurements in Rome and put up the building in St Petersburg according to them. Copies of Raphael's frescoes were commissioned from the Roman painter Christoph Unterberger, who faithfully transferred, together with his assistants, the great artist's Vatican masterpieces on to canvas. In 1787–88 the canvases were fixed in the interiors of the Raphael Loggias built by Giacomo Quarenghi in St Petersburg. The gallery consists of thirteen sections or loggias. Their walls and vaults are covered with fanciful grotesque ornaments created by Raphael under the influence of ancient paintings, which he studied during excavations of Ancient Rome. Each vault of the gallery has four paintings on biblical subjects — from the creation of the world and the story of Adam and Eve to the Crucifixion of Christ. Harmoniously included into the overall composition of the loggia, the painted images are sometimes called "Raphael's Bible". It should be mentioned that this pictorial complex was born for the second time in the middle of the nineteenth century.

49 / 50

THE RAPHAEL LOGGIAS

THE RAPHAEL LOGGIAS. DETAIL OF VAULT PAINTING

During the construction of the New Hermitage the building with the loggias was dismantled and the paintings executed in the eighteenth century on canvases were removed. The agreement with Leo von Klenze stipulated, according to the will of Nicholas I, the complete recreation of the Raphael Loggias as part of the Imperial Museum. In this way the painted copies from the great master's Vatican frescoes found a suitable place in the complex of the museum interiors. (Raphael's murals in the Vatican are, by the way, in a very poor state now.) However, the Picture Gallery did not occupy all rooms of the first floor of the New Hermitage. The entire suite of rooms running along the Raphael Loggias, from the present-day Room of Italian Majolica to the Knights' Hall and the Hall of Twelve Columns, was used to display collections of carved gems and stones and numismatics. The design of these interiors was more decorative. The polychrome painted decoration of the walls and ceilings, the reliefs and mouldings, as well as the unique inlaid parquet floors made up a fine setting for the collection of miniature glyptic works and medals. The Gallery of the History of Ancient Painting is another architectural and artistic complex of the New Hermitage, besides the Raphael Loggias, in which a cycle of monumental paintings dominates the interior decor. The walls of the gallery are adorned with 86 unique paintings executed in the ancient medium of encaustic or the application of colours with hot wax on copper plates. Produced by the Munich painter Georg Hiltensperger, they deal with events from ancient history and various legendary subjects. The pictures illustrate the origin of art in antiquity, discoveries and achievements of ancient painters, an invention of diverse techniques and technologies of painting, the flowering of art in Ancient Greece and its eventual decline in Ancient Rome during the period of the barbarians' invasions. The legendary history of art recorded on the walls of the Gallery of Ancient Painting, now largely forgotten, was, according to the architect's concept, to anticipate visitors' meeting with authentic

masterpieces of European art displayed in the first-floor rooms of the New Hermitage. The wide and gently descending State Staircase divided into three flights builds up an impressive perspective in which the white marble steps and the beautiful yellow stuccowork on the walls contrast expressively with the granite colonnades of the upper galleries. Streams of light on either side of the stairway heighten the effect to a striking resplendence. The twenty columns of Serdobolye granite support the coffered ceiling and rhythmically complete the slender and chromatically exquisite architectural composition of the upper flight and the galleries of the Main Staircase. From 1861 onwards the gallery was used for a display of the collection of Western European sculpture of the late eighteenth and early nineteenth centuries. The most remarkable exhibits among the sculptural pieces were works by the leading masters of Neo-Classicism, Antonio Canova and Berthel Thorvaldsen.

The collections of ancient art can be seen in the rooms of the ground floor specially designed for their display. Leo von Klenze is at his best in the decor of this part of the interiors. Guided by the idea to create an ultimately harmonious environment for a display of ancient and contemporary marble sculpture, decorative vases, small-scale statuary, coins, medals and gems

51 / 52

THE KNIGHTS' HALL

59

of the Ancient World, the architect subtly stylized the historical setting in which these works were originally used. For instance, the German architect placed the collections of Greek and Roman small-scale sculpture on the sides of the Main Foyer imitating the shapes of an ancient peristyle. The Dionysus Room reproduces the appearance of an ancient gallery the longitudinal walls of which are divided by powerful pillars, the floor is embellished with polychrome mosaics and the ceiling decor is stylized in the manner of ancient coffered interiors. This room, lined with red artificial marble, serves as a beautiful setting for a display of ancient white marble statues. The balance of proportions in the manner of Classical Antiquity is characteristic of sculptural pediments, showcases, sofas and armchairs intended for visitors and executed after designs by Leo von Klenze. The similar effect of a synthesis of architectural interior and museum display is also present in the Hall of Twenty Columns and the Jupiter Hall. The huge space

53 / 54

THE GALLERY OF THE HISTORY OF ANCIENT PAINTING

THE STATE (NICHOLAS) STAIRCASE

of the Jupiter Hall recalls by its scale the living apartments of the Roman emperors. The huge flat vault decorated with polychrome reliefs rests on the mighty pylons projecting from the walls. They are trimmed with artificial marble of dark grey tone in imitation of quadriums with free patterns of texture. The white marble statues of ancient gods, relief sarcophagi and busts of the Roman emperors are set up against the background of the longitudinal wall in deep recessions formed by the pylons. The overall decorative effect is enhanced thanks to the inlaid parquet floor executed in the technique of Florentine mosaics. Klenze skilfully stylized the Hall of Twenty Columns as an ancient temple by dividing the space with two rows of monumental Ionic columns. The hall was designed for a display of the collection of Greek and Etruscan vases, so Klenze included in the decor of the walls, rafters and coffers ornamental, plant and multifigured motifs inspired by ancient vase painting. A unique work of art is the mosaic floor made in the very complex Venetian *terrazzo* technique by craftsmen of the Peterhof Lapidary Works. Nowadays, the space of the Hall of Twenty Columns with slender rows of pillars is used to show graceful painted ancient vases, articles of glassware, metalwork and precious carved gems. The austere classical stylization predominant in the design of the ground floor in the New Hermitage, stresses the noble beauty of works of the ancient world and exemplifies the highest nineteenth-century accomplishment in the art of museum interior decoration.

The New Hermitage accepted its first visitors on 5 February 1852. In the first years of the museum's existence, however, admittance to the New Hermitage was strictly regimented because the newly built imperial museum, in the words of Nicholas I, was "a part and continuation of the royal residence". Therefore to enter it, guests had to receive personal invitation tickets issued by the Ministry of the Household. The New Hermitage was open daily, except Sundays and major feasts, for two or three hours a day. Between 12.30 and 2.00 in the afternoon visitors were not admitted "because at that time His Majesty wishes to visit the Hermitage each day." But soon it became easier to get to the museum, and during the reign of Alexander II the first director of the Hermitage Stepan Gedeonov obtained permission to allow free entry to all those who desired to see the imperial art collections.

55 / 56 / 57

THE DIONYSUS HALL

THE JUPITER HALL

THE NEW HERMITAGE. THE HALL OF TWENTY COLUMNS

STATUES ON THE ROOF OF THE HERMITAGE

The group of monumental decorative sculptures arranged on the balustrades of the Winter Palace's roof look like a majestic crown over the huge edifice. Created by the genius of Rastrelli, the statuary appears as a finishing touch in the Baroque decor of the façades, a symbol of Russia's imperial might and her prosperity patronized by ancient gods and heroes. Jupiter and Juno, Neptune and Amphitrite, Venus, Mars, Volcano, Minerva, Heracles and many other celebrated celestial beings, like eternal guards, are gazing from the top of the building, as if from the height of Olympus, onto the regal flow of the Neva and the pace of life in the city. On 3 November 1755, at the very beginning of construction work, Elizabeth Petrovna ordered the court architect Bartolomeo Francesco Rastrelli to begin the designing of statues and decorative vases for the balustrade of the Winter Palace. To make the statues exposed to the detrimental effects of weather more enduring, it was suggested to carve them in stone.

STATUES ON THE ROOF OF THE HERMITAGE

VIEW OF THE UNIVERSITY EMBANKMENT,
THE SPIT OF VASILYEVSKY ISLAND AND THE PETROGRAD
SIDE FROM THE ROOF OF THE WINTER PALACE

The master carver Josener Baumchen, who was responsible for this task, did a huge amount of work translating into stone the models produced by Johann Dunker after Rastrelli's drawings. The documents read that from 1756 to 1761 Baumchen carved sculpture for six pediments of the Winter Palace's façades, including "for three on the Admiralty side, and for one on the Neva side — two seated statues for each." Unfortunately time and weather proved to be detrimental for the original works of decorative sculpture. In the late nineteenth century, the semi-dilapidated stone statues gave way to new ones, made of welded copper sheets. Now the sculptural decor of the Winter Palace comprises 176 statues, the shapes and dimensions of which are ultimately close to the originals of the eighteenth century. Their expressive silhouettes crowning one of the most renowned edifices in St Petersburg attest to the glory of the Winter Palace in the splendid panorama of the Palace Embankment.

THE GENERAL STAFF BUILDING

The present-day Hermitage is a dynamically developing museum centre justly considered one of the largest in the world. The constantly growing collections of the Hermitage, its active exhibiting and educational activities demand the enlargement of its premises. In keeping with the present-day concept of the museum's development, the "Great Hermitage" project has been worked out — the largest museum project in Russia for the past hundred years. It presumes a transfer to the Hermitage of several buildings around Palace Square. United by underground passages, they will make up a single complex with the now functioning buildings of the museum. In the 1990s the Hermitage began a reconstruction of the eastern wing of the General Staff building put up in 1820–27 by the architect Carlo Rossi. The majestic classical edifice formed a mighty arc skirting Palace Square from the south and creating a harmonious ensemble with the powerful Baroque façade of the Winter Palace. The stately arch crowned with a monumental chariot of Glory links the two wings of the General Staff building. In the nineteenth century the left wing

61 / 62 / 63

THE ARCH OF THE GENERAL STAFF BUILDING

PANORAMIC VIEW OF PALACE SQUARE
AND THE GENERAL STAFF BUILDING

THE ALEXANDER COLUMN. THE ANGEL

of the building housed the Ministry of Foreign Affairs — the offices and living apartments of the minister, Count Karl Nesselrode, Chancellor of the Russian Empire. It was for him and his wife that Carlo Rossi decorated the suite of state rooms and private apartments. The surviving historical interiors designed in the Empire style are adorned with elegant paintings, moulded ornaments, mirrors and inlaid parquet floors. The magnificent rooms and halls are now used for displays of various art collections from the stocks of the Hermitage.

The Great Hermitage of the twenty-first century will become the core of a multifunctional museum space open for all forms of contact with the treasures of art and culture. The large-scale project includes exhibition galleries, lecture halls, a theatre and libraries, a computer information centre with diverse educational and entertainment programmes, book and antique shops, cafés and restaurants. All these and many other facilities will make up a sort of a Universe providing the visitor of the new century with an opportunity to enjoy all kinds of aesthetic experience and cultural leisure.

THE HERMITAGE

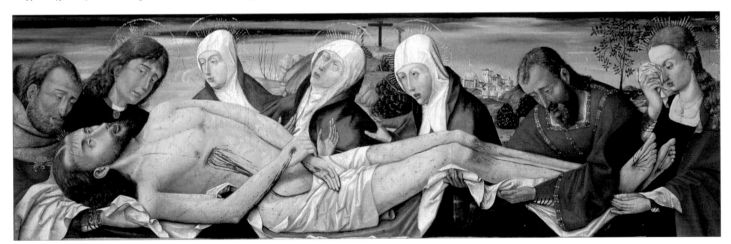

ITALY

THE NETHERLANDS

FRANCE

SPAIN

The Hermitage, generally acknowledged to be one of the richest museums in the world, is held to have been created in 1764. In that year the Berlin merchant Johann Ernest Gotzkowsky offered to the Russian court, in payment of his debt, a collection of 225 paintings, mainly works by seventeenth-century Dutch and Flemish artists. This collection made up the core of the newly established gallery of the Russian Empress Catherine the Great. At the end of the 1760s the Hermitage collection continued to grow rapidly. In the summer of 1769 more than 600 works of art, formerly owned by the Saxon minister Heinrich Brühl, arrived in St Petersburg from Dresden. In 1772 the Empress's agents succeeded, as a result of secret dealings, to bring to St Petersburg the exceedingly valuable collection of Pierre Crozat, evading its sale at an auction. A real sensation for the European artistic world became the purchase by the Russian Empress in 1779 of the collection of Sir Robert Walpole that included masterpieces by Rubens, Van Dyck, Poussin and Murillo. By the end of the eighteenth century the picture gallery of Catherine the Great could rival the best collections of Europe. According to the inventory compiled in 1797, it comprised about 4,000 works. Remaining a private palatial collection, the gallery was at the same time accessible to spectators. Admittance to see the collection was given to foreigners on a visit to Russia as well as to artists and students of the Academy of Arts. In addition to paintings, the Empress's collection included a large number of engravings and drawings, as well as tapestries, carved gems, ivories, items of faience, glass, bronze, silver and gold. The death of Catherine the Great marked the end of the first, most active period in the establishment of the museum. In the nineteenth century the imperial museum's holdings were enlarged with the famous collection of Spanish painting purchased from the Amsterdam banker Baron Coesevelt (1814), the collection of Napoleon's first wife Joséphine de Beauharnais (1815), as well as a large number of valuable Italian paintings accumulated by the Barbarigo family in Venice (1850). After that the gallery did not receive any subtsantial funds for the acquisition of large collections. In the second half of the nineteenth and early twentieth century the Hermitage collection was enriched mainly with individual masterpieces by great European masters as well

as with collections bequeathed to the museum by their owners. At the beginning of the twentieth century the Hermitage became the largest scientific museum centre in Europe. However, the beginning of the First World War broke the regular routine of activities in the museum in which priceless treasures were preserved. The capital of Russia was in a dangerous proximity to the front and therefore it was decided to take some part of the collection to Moscow. Soon after the October Revolution and the establishment of Soviet power, thanks to the energetic measures undertaken by the Council of the Hermitage, organized in 1918, the bulk of the evacuated treasures was returned. All the display rooms were opened for visitors on 2 January 1923 and this was an important event in the life of the city. Meanwhile, numerous works from nationalized private collections began to arrive in the Hermitage. This period, however, was associated not only with sizeable additions to the collection but with dramatic losses too. In the 1920s, the Hermitage had to transfer 500 works, mostly important displayed exhibits, to the Museum of Fine Arts in Moscow. Some of famous "pairs" were disunited – for example, *Boy with a Dog* by Murillo was left in the Hermitage, while its companion piece, *Girl with Fruit*, was sent to Moscow; Poussin's *Battle of the Israelites and Amalekites* and *Battle of the Israelites and Amorites* were also divided between the two museums. At the end of the 1920s barbarous sales of the best paintings in the Hermitage collections to foreign countries began. The Soviet state was in urgent need of money for the restoration of its economy devastated by the war and revolution. The authorities decided to raise money in the simplest and seemingly most reliable way – by selling the Hermitage's treasures. At first, works by second-rate artists and pieces of decorative arts were sent in great secrecy to auctions and to private collections in the West. However, the received funds proved to be insufficient and in the early 1930s many priceless Hermitage treasures were sold through the major Western collectors dealing with Soviet Russia – the head of Iraqi Petroleum Company Galust Gulbenkyan, the American millionaire Armand Hammer and the U.S. Minister of Finance Mellon. As a result the Hermitage lost, among many other works, two masterpieces by Raphael, The *Alba Madonna* and *St George*, *The Adoration of the Magi* by Botticelli, *Venus before the Mirror* by Titian, works by Veronese and Perugino. From the 1930s onwards, the Hermitage had very few acquisitions. An exclusion was the transfer in 1930–34 of thirty paintings by the French Impressionists and Post-Impressionists from the Museum of New Western Art in Moscow. In 1941 the Hermitage treasures faced one more serious trial. Soon after the beginning of the war St Petersburg, then Leningrad, became a front-line city again. The Hermitage's collections were quickly evacuated again, this time to Sverdlovsk. Immediately after lifting the siege of the city, in January 1944, the Hermitage began to get alive. The collections taken away to the Urals came back and the activities of the museum began to revive. In 1948 the museum received 298 canvases by artists of the late nineteenth and early twentieth centuries from the liquidated Museum of New Western Art in Moscow. Among them were priceless works by the French Impressionists, Matisse and Picasso, as well as several canvases by Wassily Kandinsky. The purchases of works by famous masters of the twentieth century, Chaïm Soutine, Maurice Utrillo, Raoul Dufy and Aristide Maillol, at sales in Paris in the late 1990s shows that the museum established by Catherine the Great continues to develop.

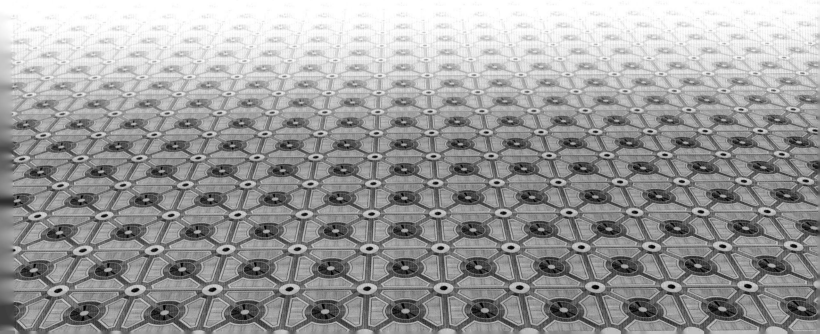

ITALY

The collection of Italian art occupies more than thirty rooms and halls of the Hermitage and rivals the leading collections of the world. The Hermitage is justly proud of its masterpieces dating from the High Renaissance — the works of Leonardo da Vinci, Raphael, Giorgione, Titian and Michelangelo, a vast collection of first-rate paintings from the seventeenth and eighteenth centuries, a unique group of *bozzetti* (terracotta studies) by Gianlorenzo Bernini and a superb assemblage of decorative and applied art. Well represented in the Hermitage are pieces of sculpture dating from the late eighteenth and early nineteenth centuries — a period of Italian Neo-Classicism, primarily the works of Antonio Canova. The museum has also a small collection of twentieth-century Italian art including two still lifes by Giorgio Morandi, sculptures by Giacomo Manzù, Emilio Greco and Francesco Messina. Chronologically the Italian Renaissance divides into two unequal phases. The early period, known as the Quattrocento, covers the fifteenth century. The High Renaissance (from the late 15th century to the 1530s) is characterized by the highest achievements of Raphael, Leonardo da Vinci and Michelangelo. In Venice, the period of the High Renaissance, associated with the work of Titian and his followers, continued almost throughout the sixteenth century. The Early Renaissance was preceded by a phase which lasted more than a century and to which the Renaissance largely owed its great spiritual discoveries — the so-called Proto-Renaissance. It was at the end of the thirteenth century that radical changes took place both in the economic and spiritual spheres of Italian life. In independent Italian city-states, which became free from old feudal relations, there emerged

a new ideology — Humanism, with man as the focus of its attention. Unlike medieval asceticism that ignored all earthly and corporeal, Humanist philosophers considered man to be God's most perfect creation and asserted his endless spiritual and physical possibilities. In this sense they were close to ancient philosophy with its cult of beautiful man, God's prototype. Classical culture became a model for study and imitation in Italy during this period, hence the term "Renaissance" — a revival of the artistic traditions of Classical Antiquity. Art flowered in Italian cities and local rulers encouraged the process. Each major centre had its own artistic school bringing talented masters together. Centres of new, Renaissance culture emerged in Siena, Florence, Venice, Umbria, Ferrari and Rome. The Hermitage's collection of the Italian exhibits dating from the early phase of the Renaissance is not very large. The works by artists of this period, who became known as the "Primitives", still betray the traditions of European Gothic and Byzantine icon-painting — the two powerful elements of medieval art. Giotto, a great fourteenth-century reformer, breathed life into the religious canon making fleshless characters of medieval painting more material and alive. Practically all artists of his time owe something to Giotto, and the paintings in the Hermitage collection give a vivid picture of the struggle between the obsolete medieval dogmas and the new Renaissance worldview in the fourteenth and early fifteenth centuries. *The Crucifixion with St Mary and St John*, created in the second half of the fifteenth century by the Florentine painter Niccolo di Pietro Gerini (mentioned between 1350 and 1415), was listed in the manuscript catalogue

THE NEW HERMITAGE
THE SMALL ITALIAN SKYLIGHT ROOM

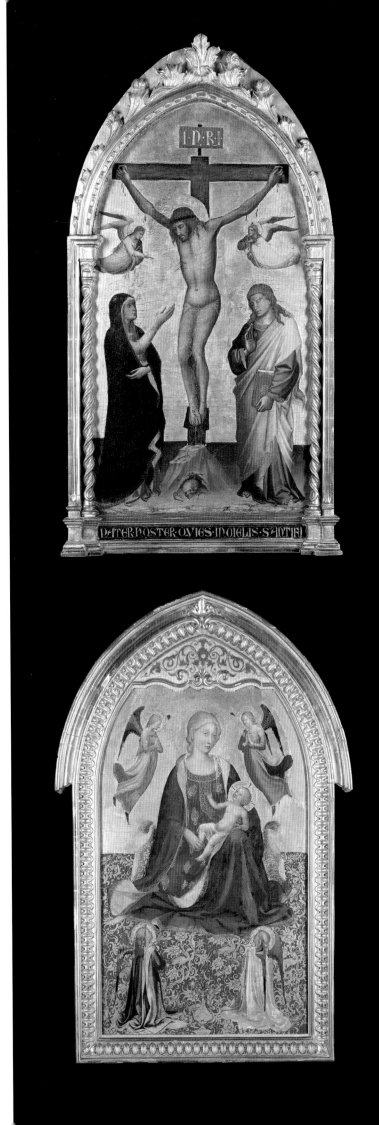

of the Count Pavel Stroganov collection (whence it came to the Hermitage) as a work by of one of Giotto's followers. The traditions of medieval Byzantine painting are still strongly felt in the conventional treatment of the figures depicted on a flat golden meadow, in the symmetry and balance of the composition. According to the Byzantine canon, the figure of Christ, nailed to the transverse beam of the Cross, is placed strictly in the centre; to the left of it is the mourning Madonna and to the right the Apostle John, traditionally portrayed with a book in his hand. The Latin letters *I.N.R.I.* over the Crucifix denote the name and guilt of the executed person — *Iesus Nasarenus Rex Iudaeorum* (Jesus of Nazareth, King of the Jews). At the foot of the Crucifix, at an elevation symbolizing Calvary, is represented the skull of the biblical Adam who was buried, according to the Church tradition, under Golgotha. The gilded Gothic frame bears the inscription: *PATER. NOSTER.QVIES.INCIELIS.SANTIFI* (Our Father living in the Heavens). The image of the Madonna, the right-hand panel from the *Annunciation* diptych by Simone Martini, the leading artist of the fifteenth-century Sienese school, suggests a noticeable medieval Gothic influence. The left-hand wing of the altarpiece showing the Archangel Gabriel is now at the National Gallery in Washington. Traditionally St Mary was supposed to look feared and embarrassed on seeing the Archangel, but Simone Martini succeeded in conveying this state with an exquisite and even secular grace. Francesco Petrarch, a great Renaissance poet, very keenly felt this aspect of the master's creative gift and devoted the following lines to his friend:

> My Simone was perhaps in Paradise,
> Whence the noble Virgin descended,
> He saw her there and portrayed on the parchment...

64 / 65 / 66

NICCOLO DI PIETRO GERINI. *Ca* 1350–1415
THE CRUCIFIXION WITH ST MARY AND ST JOHN
Between 1368 and 1415
Tempera on panel. 85.5 x 52.7 cm

FRA GIOVANNI DA FIESOLE (FRA ANGELICO).
Ca 1400–1455
THE MADONNA AND CHILD WITH ANGELS. *Ca* 1425
Tempera on panel. 80 x 51 cm

SIMONE MARTINI. *Ca* 1284–1344
THE MADONNA FROM THE *ANNUNCIATION* SCENE
Tempera on panel. 30.5 x 21.5 cm

67

FRA GIOVANNI DA FIESOLE
(FRA ANGELICO). *Ca* 1400–1455
**THE MADONNA AND CHILD WITH ST DOMINIC
AND ST THOMAS AQUINAS.** 1424–30
Fresco. 196 x 187 cm

68 / 69

FILIPPINO LIPPI. *Ca* 1457–1504
THE ADORATION OF THE INFANT CHRIST. Mid-1480s
Oil on copper plate, transferred from a panel
Diameter 53 cm

LORENZO COSTA. 1460–1535
PORTRAIT OF A WOMAN. Early 1500s
Tempera and oil on canvas. 57 x 44 cm

Fra Beato Angelico da Fiesole (Guido di Pietro), one of the most poetic and elevated artists of the Early Renaissance, took monastic vows and spent his entire life in endless toil, painting holy images permeated with a bright religious feeling on the walls of monasteries near Florence. The "angelic" name itself given to him in the monastery reflects the attitude of the famous master's contemporaries to his art. Fra Beato's works belongs to the Quattrocento, but the features of medieval convention are still prominent in his paintings. *The Madonna and Child with Angels* is very close in style to the traditional treatment of the subject popular in Florence at the turn of the centuries. The painting produces a colourful, even decorative impression created by the Virgin's red and blue clothes, the soft radiance of the Angels' wings and the elaborate ornaments of the foot of the throne against the brilliant gold of the background. The elegant vessel with lilies placed in the lower part of the painting is an allusion to Virgin Mary's purity. It might seem that the delightful example of Fra Beato's work is wholly linked with the old tradition. However, the new, Renaissance features are evident in the treatment of volumes: the fair-haired Madonna is already not only a spiritual ideal but a real-life woman, too, and the real proportions of her body are traceable under the folds of the cloak.

Another famous work by Fra Beato Angelico — the monumental fresco *The Madonna and Child with St Dominic and St Thomas Aquinas* (1424–30) — is also devoted to the Virgin Mary. This is in fact the central part of the painted decoration of the Monastery of St Dominic at Fiesole, where the artist worked in the 1420s. Its subject — the Madonna seated on the throne and flanked by saints — is derived from the medieval tradition and is called *sacra conversazione*, but the artist endows the images of the saints with a more concrete, in comparison with the medieval treatment, almost individual characterization. The figures of the Madonna and the saints seem to be three-dimensional, palpable against the light-blue background of the fresco imitating space. However, the colour scheme of Fra Beato's wall paintings looked differently in the fifteenth century — it was established in the process of restoration that originally the background had been not blue but red with golden stars. In the second half of the nineteenth century the monastery was closed, the valuable murals cut out and sold. The fresco with the Madonna became the property of two Florentine painters from whom it was acquired for the Imperial Hermitage in 1882. In the fifteenth century Florence occupied the leading position among Italian art schools. Artists, who were encouraged at the court of Duke Lorenzo de' Medici, known as Lorenzo the

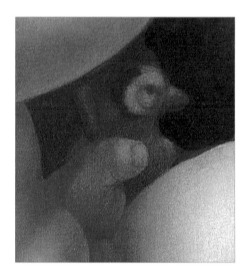

Magnificent, created masterpieces of paintings, sculpture and architecture. The marble relief *The Madonna and Child* by the Florentine sculptor Antonio Rosselino is remarkable for the virtuoso mastery of carving — the marble vibrates in numerous colour tints like a painted work, and the light sliding softly over the surface of the material stresses the unusual harmony and spiritual elevation of the images of the Madonna and the Infant Christ. Filippino Lippi, one of the leading masters of the Florentine Quattrocento, is represented in the Hermitage by two works, the tondo *The Adoration of the Infant Christ* and a painting with the *Annunciation* scene. Both works are notable for a refined subtlety of taste and a special elegance that distinguishes masters of the Florentine Renaissance in the last decades of the fifteenth century.

The most celebrated masterpieces in the Hermitage collections — two paintings by Leonardo da Vinci, eight works by Titian and one sculpture by Michelangelo — belong to the High Renaissance, a short brilliant period in Italian art that lasted less than fifty years. The great Leonardo da Vinci was born near Florence, in the small village of Vinci, hence his name. He revealed his genius not only in painting but also in science, technical

70 / 71 / 72

LEONARDO DA VINCI. 1452–1519
THE LITTA MADONNA. *1470 – ca* 1490–91
Tempera on canvas, transferred from a panel
42 x 33 cm

sphere, music, philosophy and literature. Leonardo started to work on the Hermitage's *Madonna and Child* at the end of the 1470s when he was employed by Lodovico Moro, the Duke of Milan. Leonardo used the medium of tempera traditional for Italy. Later the picture came to be also known as *The Litta Madonna* after the name of its first owner — the Milanese Count Antoine Litta. The composition of the painting is so thoroughly thought out and balanced that this small-scale piece produces a truly monumental impression. The triangle, into which the figures of the Madonna and the Child can be inscribed, emphasizes the ideal balance and majestic simplicity of this outwardly everyday scene, as well as a profound symbolism of its subject matter. The Virgin's glance is directed at the Child Christ, the corners of her lips are touched by a barely noticeable smile. This is one of Leonardo's favourite devices intended to show his personages' introspection, mysterious aloofness. The Child's gaze, in turn, is directed at the viewer conveying, as it were, His presentiment of the torments. The goldfinch in the Child's hand has the same allusion — the red colour of the bird's head symbolizes the drops of Christ's blood to be spilt for mankind. *The Madonna with Flower* or *The Benois Madonna*, as it is otherwise called after its last owner, the Russian architect Leonty Benois, is the great artist's early work. Painted in 1478, it is one of Leonardo's few indubitable works. Many details in this canvas, executed in the medium

73 / 74 / 75

LEONARDO DA VINCI. 1452–1519
**THE MADONNA WITH A FLOWER
(THE BENOIS MADONNA).** 1478
Oil on canvas, transferred from a panel
49.5 x 31.5 cm

→
FRANCESCO MELZI. 1493 – *ca* 1570
PORTRAIT OF A WOMAN. *Ca* 1520
Oil on canvas, transferred from a panel. 76 x 63 cm

76

RAPHAEL (RAFFAELLO SANTI). 1483–1520
THE CONESTABILE MADONNA
Late 1502 – early 1503
Tempera on canvas, transferred from a panel
17.5 x 18 cm

of oils unusual for that period, echo the traditions of the Quattrocento. The artist, however, treats the subject in a more free and sweeping manner. Leonardo depicts the Madonna as a young Florentine woman wearing a fashionable dress and playing with her child. Such genre interpretation of a religious theme was not unusual for the fifteenth century. The symbolism of the painting is also traditional: the mother stretches to her baby the four-petal flower that alludes to the form of the Cross; over the heads of the Madonna and the Child are thin golden haloes. At the same time Leonardo decisively breaks the tradition — the colours of the Madonna's garments are unusual and her lovely smiling face is far from the ideal of beauty.

The artist was more concerned here with the nuances of vivid facial expressions.

The art of the great Leonardo exerted an enormous influence on his contemporaries. His faithful pupils, having thoroughly studied his manner of painting, often copied the master's pieces and employed Leonardo's stylistic devices in their own works. As a result their paintings were often ascribed to the great artist himself and were even treated as his veritable masterpieces. Such is the case with the Hermitage's *Flora* produced by Leonardo's favourite pupil Francesco Melzi. *Flora* or *Columbine* (from the name of the flower, columbine, in the model's hand) entered the Hermitage in 1850 as a work by Leonardo da Vinci. Nobody doubted the attribution until the 1960s. There even exist research works that convincingly prove the authorship of the genius of the Renaissance. Today, however, it is exactly known that the painting was executed by Melzi, but each of its details bespeaks that this is a large and rather skillful "quotation" from the great Leonardo's oeuvre. Raphael (Rafaello Santi) was second to Leonardo neither in fame nor in excellence. During his short lifetime Raphael succeeded in painting dozens of masterpieces — superb examples of the High Renaissance. It was Raphael who initiated large-scale wall painting in this period, as is testified by the murals in the papal apartments of the Vatican. The Hermitage copy of the Vatican's Loggia by Raphael give some idea about the Roman period of the artist's creative career, the period of his ultimate accomplishments, revealing his sweep of fantasy, freedom of handling

77 / 78

**FEMALE PORTRAIT
(LAURA THE BEAUTIFUL).** 1460s
Cameo. Sardonyx. 2.0 x 1.3 cm

APOLLO SLAYING A PYTHON. 16th century
Cameo. Milan
By Alessandro Masnago. Agate

79 / 80

WEDDING BOWL "CAMILLA LA BELLA"
16th century. Majolica

DISH. 16th century
Deruta. Majolica

84

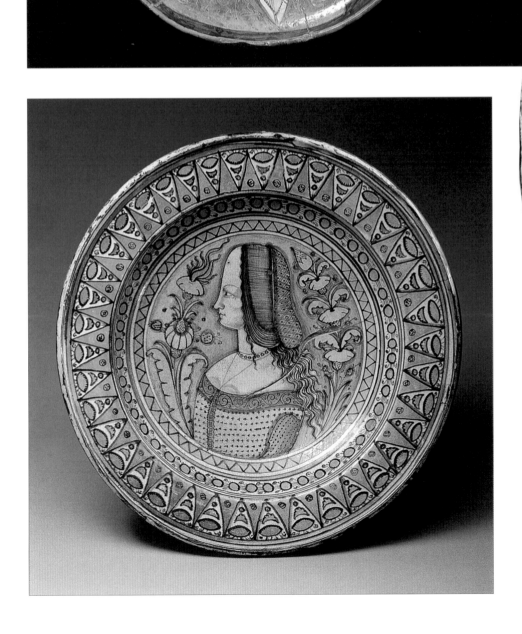

and typically Renaissance balance of composition. The two authentic paintings by Raphael in the Hermitage collection date from the early 1500s. *The Conestabile Madonna* was evidently executed at the end of 1502 or beginning of 1503, when the artist still lived in his native Perugia. *The Holy Family*, or *The Madonna with the Beardless St Joseph*, is datable to 1506.

The small-size, almost miniature-like *Conestabile Madonna* (the picture's title comes from the name of its former owner) has the shape of a tondo, i.e. the composition is placed within a circle. The rhythm of basic details in the painting is subordinate to its circular outline. The figure of the Madonna, with the Child in her lap, stands out in a clear-cut silhouette against a wide panoramic landscape with a soft undulating line of hills on the horizon, smooth lakes and the thin trunks of slender trees. The spring weather is an emotional setting for the image of the mother, as youthful and pure as the world around her. The painting is mounted in a luxurious gilt frame that once formed a single whole with the panel on which the painting was executed, and must have been produced after a drawing by the artist himself. The age of the Renaissance distinguished itself by the supreme level of workmanship in all kinds of art. Magnificent Italian *palazzi* were adorned, in addition to painting and sculpture, with numerous and varied objects of decorative art. The Hermitage owns about five hundred superb examples of majolica — dishes, vases and other vessels. Of particular interest are the so-called "wedding dishes" or "plates for lovers". In the centre of the bright-coloured dish, decorated with a polychrome ornament, was usually placed a half-length female representation skirted by a band with the name of the girl.

The beautiful Venice, the gem of the Adriatic, stepped on the path of the Renaissance somewhat later than Tuscany, Umbria or Siena. The distinctive feature of the Venetian school of painting was its particularly keen attention to colour.

81 / 82

PALMA VECCHIO
(JACOPO NEGRETTI). 1480–1528
PORTRAIT OF A MAN. Between 1512 and 1515
Oil on canvas. 93.5 x 72 cm

GIORGIONE (GIORGIO DA CASTELFRANCO). 1478(?)–1510
JUDITH. 1500s
Oil on canvas, transferred from a panel. 144 x 66.5 cm

The very atmosphere of the city saturated with the richest combinations and subtlest nuances of colour encouraged artists to capture the pictorial wealth of the world. This specific quality distinguishes great Venetian painters. Giorgione (Giorgio da Castelfranco) was one of those who brought the Renaissance to Venice in the early sixteenth century. The biography of this outstanding Venetian painter has many vague moments to this day: he never signed his works and no more than ten works are definitely ascribed to him today, although some scholars increase this number to several dozens. The date of the artist's birth is also unknown — the only available fact is that he died in his early thirties during the epidemic of plague in 1510.

The Hermitage owns one of Giorgione's masterpieces   his *Judith*. The biblical story tells about the feat of a young Jewish woman who saved her city attacked by the Assyrian troops headed by Holofernes. Judith secretly penetrated to the enemy's camp and charmed the army leader by her beauty. After a feast, during the night, she decapitated Holofernes. According to the humanist idea of the Renaissance, the man or woman who made a feat for the sake of his people, was beautiful both spiritually and physically, and therefore the image of Judith was exceedingly popular in Italian art. Giorgione's Judith is strikingly calm after her terrible murder — she has no doubts and is convinced in her righteousness. Stiffened next to the enemy's cut-off head, she tramples on the terrible "pedestal" betraying no symptoms of unease or disquiet. The painting is full of contrasts enhancing the impression it produces. The beautiful face of the girl is set in opposition to Holofernes' features distorted by the grimace of death. The body and garments of Judith are rendered in a typically Venetian gamut of colours — warm pinks and cold greens. These tints endow the protagonist's image with a special harmony and ease which is stressed by the massive trunk of a mighty old tree.

83 / 84

TITIAN (TIZIANO VECELLIO). 1485/90–1576
DANAË. Between 1546 and 1553
Oil on canvas. 120 x 187 cm

TITIAN (TIZIANO VECELLIO). 1485/90–1576
PORTRAIT OF A YOUNG WOMAN. 1530s
Oil on canvas. 96 x 75 cm

Giorgione's masterpiece came to the Hermitage from the French collection of Pierre Crozat, Baron de Thiers, as the work of the "divine" Raphael. Titian (Tiziano Vecellio), the leader of the Venetian school during its greatest period, started his creative career in Giorgione's workshop. The Venetians revered their compatriot who lived a long life and never ceased to amaze them by his mastery. The Hermitage has eight paintings by Titian, almost all of them from his mature period. Titian, who became the official painter of the Venetian Republic in 1516, created portraits and multifigured compositions of then popular mythological and biblical themes. The colours in his works are permeated with light and saturated with hues — they not just "colour" objects but make up the

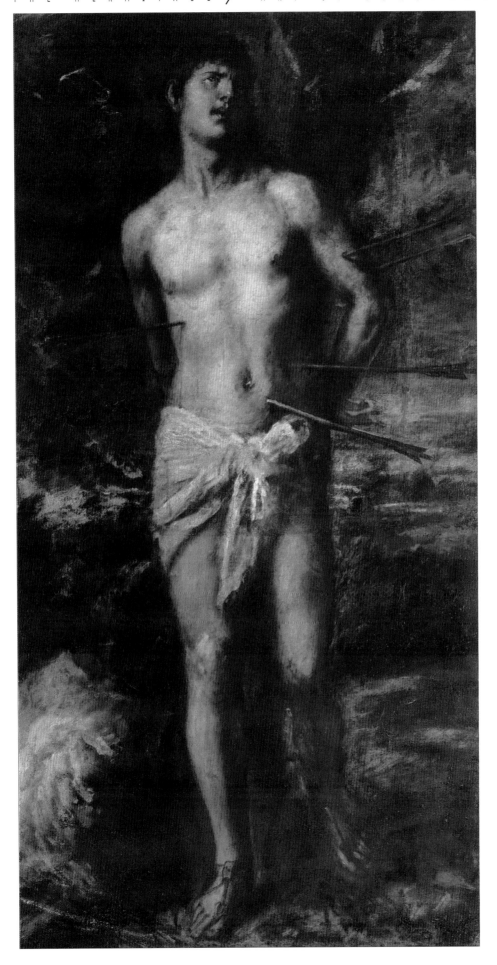

very essence of the things depicted turning into silver, valuable textiles, the sky or a beautiful female body. The name of the young Venetian depicted in Titian's *Portrait of a Young Woman* is not known. This is the artist's favourite type embodying his ideal of beauty. Titian's quiet, golden-haired and corpulent women — nude ancient heroines, biblical characters and his contemporaries wearing fashionable garments — all are natural, dignified and self-confident, regarding themselves, as it were, God's perfect creations. The naked female body was for Titian an inexhaustible source of rich chromatic relationships. The Hermitage's *Danaë* is one of several versions painted by the artist — he returned to this mythological image several times, translating into colour his admiration for woman's beauty. According to an ancient Greek myth, an oracle prophesied to Acricius, King of Argos, that his grandson would kill him. Trying to evade death, Acrisius imprisoned the beautiful Danaë, his only daughter, into a brazen tower and doomed her for lonely life. The young girl, however, was seen by Zeus, the ruler of the Olympian gods, who came under the spell of her beauty and penetrated into the tower impregnable for mortals in the form of a shower of gold. Titian was not exact in his rendition of the mythological subject — his lovely heroine looks again like a beautiful Venetian woman. The luminous whiteness of her body is highlighted by the deep reddish shades of the bed-curtain and coverlet, the servant's olive-green clothes, the greyish-golden clouds through which the face of Zeus and the glistening

85 / 86

TITIAN (TIZIANO VECELLIO). 1485/90–1576
ST SEBASTIAN. *Ca* 1570
Oil on canvas. 210 x 115 cm

TITIAN (TIZIANO VECELLIO). 1485/90–1576
THE REPENTANT MARY MAGDALENE. 1560s
Oil on canvas. 118 x 97 cm

shower of golden coins can be seen, and the blue distance of the background landscape. *Danaë* is dated from the turn of the 1540s and 1550s, the years when a new, more dramatic period in Titian's creative career began. Now the artist saw not only beauty and harmony in the world, but tragedy, struggle and death, too. This led to a change in his pictorial manner. His style of painting grew more sophisticated, even more saturated with shades, and his wide impasto strokes seemed to reflect the artist's state of soul. *The Repentant Mary Magdalene* painted in this period is Titian's acknowledged masterpiece. The Hermitage canvas features St Mary in a moment of her passionate prayer. The image of the beautiful golden-haired Venetian woman is endowed with exceedingly turbulent dramatic feelings conveyed through a brilliant accord of sonorous and deep tones, through the varying brushstrokes, now soft and vibrant and now thick and energetic. Titian's techniques show a striking freedom of handling in his later works. He improvizes with a colour surface loading it with an impasto, almost palpable layer of colour and coating it with semitransparent glazings which yield a singularly picturesque effect. The artist's palette does not show much variety — on the contrary, his colours are close to one another, almost monochrome. Another masterpiece by Titian in the Hermitage collection, *St Sebastian*,

87 /88

PAOLO VERONESE. 1528–1588
THE ADORATION OF THE MAGI. Early 1570s
Oil on copper plate. 45 x 34.5 cm

TINTORETTO (JACOPO ROBUSTI). 1518–1594
THE BIRTH OF ST JOHN THE BAPTIST. *Ca* 1550
Oil on canvas. 181 x 266 cm

was painted by the artist during the last decade of his lifetime. It is difficult to believe that this tragic image is the work of a ninety-year-old man. The huge canvas is painted in dynamic brushstrokes pervaded with energy; the surface is literally modelled "by the painter's fingers rather than by his brush". According to legend, the Romans sentenced the young Sebastian who preached Christianity to an excruciating torment — he was made a living target for archers. Titian portrays the saint during the moment of his death: his beautiful, strong, classically proportioned body is pierced with arrows; his suffering glance is aspiring to the heavens. The painting has no traditional division into a forefront and background, the figure is set in space and is part of the unified light and air medium in which everything is inter-related and inseparable.

Jacopo Tintoretto — a major representative of the so-called Late Renaissance — continued the traditions of Titian's painting in the second half of the sixteenth century. Jacopo Robusti, known as Tintoretto (he was born into the family of a dyer — his surname means a "small dyer" in Italian), began his career in the workshop of Titian. However, soon the pupil of the great master went to Rome where he familiarized himself with the work of Michelangelo. From that time onwards his painting combined the two ways laid by the titans of the Renaissance: the power and expressiveness of Michelangelo's drawing and Titian's exceptionally rich colour range. The Hermitage has only one doubtless work by Tintoretto — *The Birth of St John the Baptist*. The artist treats the Gospel subject as a mundane genre scene in a full agreement with the Venetian Renaissance tradition. The space of the painting is filled with servants and wet-nurses bustling around the newly born child. They wear luxurious, *décolleté* dresses which were fashionable with young ladies during the artist's lifetime. St Mary, the future mother of Christ, holding the Infant St John in her hands, is singled out in the female group only by a halo shining over her head. Placed in the foreground are copper wash-basins, and the red cat is on the watch for the hen carelessly walking along the marble plaques of the floor. And only Zechariah who is engrossed in prayer seemingly does not take care of the turbulent movement reigning the scene. This painting, still largely of a Renaissance kind in its manner, betrays some features that are to develop fully in the seventeenth century: the monumental dynamic expression of the Baroque and the special realistic genre quality that was characteristic of Caravaggio and his followers.

The fundamental principles of the Baroque style, the leading trend of European art in the seventeenth century, were laid in the work of the great Renaissance master Michelangelo (Michelangelo Bounarroti), an outstanding sculptor, architect, painter and poet. Almost all the best works

89 / 90

MICHELANGELO BUONARROTI. 1475–1564
THE CROUCHING BOY. *Ca* 1530
Marble. Height 54 cm

CARAVAGGIO. 1571–1610
THE LUTE PLAYER. *Ca* 1595
Oil on canvas. 94 x 119 cm

91 / 92 / 93

FRANCESCO GUARDI. 1712–1793
VIEW OF SAN GIORGIO MAGGIORE ISLAND IN VENICE
Oil on canvas. 44 x 60 cm

GIOVANNI BATTISTA TIEPOLO. 1696–1770
**MAECENAS PRESENTING THE LIBERAL ARTS
TO EMPEROR AUGUSTUS.** *Ca* 1745
Oil on canvas. 69.5 x 89 cm

ANTONIO CANALE (CANALETTO). 1697–1768
**A RECEPTION OF THE FRENCH AMBASSADOR
IN VENICE.** 1740s
Oil on canvas. 181 x 259.5 cm

by the artist are now in his native Italy. The only example of his sculptural legacy in the Hermitage collection, *The Crouching Boy*, dates to the later period of his creative career and is probably connected with his work at the Medici' Capella in Florence. This small marble piece clearly shows the master's typical creative device characteristic of his best sculptural works. Michelangelo had a perfect command of the carver's art — by carving the stone and removing the unnecessary material he made real the concept of the image that had emerged in his imagination. Such method demanded from the sculptor an impeccable inner feeling. The great master saw the essence of the sculptor's labour in releasing the conceived shape from its stone "shell". Michelangelo's figures are strong and athletic; the surface of the stone which is often left partly unpolished, rough in his later works, emphasizes the powerful muscles and massive proportions. The bent body is reminiscent of a tightly twisted spring charged with immense energy. At the same time the boy's facial features, arms and feet are barely suggested and his body is tragically bound in torpid arrest. The boy's complex emotional state which combines suffering, concentration and introspection is conveyed through the rhythm of the sculptural masses and through the expressive play of light and shade on the hollows and swells of the marble block.

Many sixteenth-century Italian artists contributed to the emergence of the Baroque — a powerful artistic movement which dominated the European art scene in the seventeenth century. The leading figure among them was Caravaggio (Michelangelo Merisi da Caravaggio), a great innovator of Italian art. Caravaggio put in the centre of his paintings real people and life around them. It is primarily with him that a special democratic tendency in European art, a distinct sort of realism that became widespread in the seventeenth century, is associated. The dynamism and emotional tension of his monumental canvases laid the basis for the stylistic principles of Baroque painting. Caravaggio's formative influence on his contemporaries could be compared only with the impact exercised on the art of their times by the titans of the Renaissance. The only Caravaggio in the Hermitage collection, *The Lute Player*, vividly exemplifies the Italian painter's original artistic manner. Using the device of enhancing the contrasts of light and shade, he attains a great sense of volume, an almost illusory material, three-dimensional quality of the pictorial form. The lovely, tender, distinctive face of the young musician, the almost feminine elegance of his hands, the soft outlines of the neck

and shoulders stress the model's individuality. The fruit, music, violin and flowers are painted with a great attention to detail. This seemingly unassuming genre scene bears, however, a latent allegorical message which was characteristic of genre painting in the seventeenth century. Youth and beauty are but fleeting — this is suggested in the picture by the broken string of the bow and a crack on the table-top. The fruit and flowers are yet fresh but soon they will wrinkle and dry out; music itself is only a transient moment disappearing in a stream of time.

In the eighteenth century only one Italian art school, that of Venice, was at the height of its flowering. The beautiful city did not suffer from the military or economic trials which badly influenced the cultural processes in other parts of Italy. Venice had remained an independent aristocratic republic until the invasion of Napoleon's troops. It looked like a glistening world in which endless carnivals and luxurious pageants succeeded one another. The most celebrated Venetian master of the eighteenth century was Giovanni Battista Tiepolo, one of the last outstanding monumental painter of Italy. The five large-scale paintings in the Hermitage collection based on subjects form ancient history were intended for the decoration of a hall in the palace of the Dolfino family in Venice. This series created in the 1720s, when Tiepolo was not even thirty years old, is amazing for its virtuosity and maturity of execution. The artist's small-scale allegoric painting *Maecenas Presenting the Liberal Arts to Emperor Augustus* appears modest next to his majestic monumental paintings at first glance, but it is precisely this work that gives a full notion about his mastery as a painter. The subject of the work is connected with the real historical figure — the Roman senator Gaius Cilnius Maecenas who became so famous for his patronage of artists that his name became a common noun. The picture was commissioned by Count Algarotti and dedicated to the celebration of Augustus III, Elector of Saxony. It belongs to Tiepolo's mature period and is remarkable for the unusual wealth and freshness of its colour range.

The last great figure of classical Italian art was Antonio Canova, the founder of Neo-Classicism in European sculpture of the late eighteenth and early nineteenth centuries. Infatuation with ancient art began in Europe as early as the 1760s. An impetus for this interest was given by sensational archaeological discoveries on the sites of two ancient Roman towns — Pompeii and Herculaneum. In search of the beautiful ideal European artists again turned to Classical Antiquity — the golden age of art. Works by Canova perfectly reflect the ideal of the era. They are remarkable for a harmony of proportions, beauty of line and consummate grace. The Hermitage owns fifteen marble statues by this artist who became an idol of art patrons and collectors in his lifetime. In his sculptural composition *Cupid and Psyche* Canova turned to the myth which was widespread in Neo-Classical art. The sculptor succeeded in finding a striking rhythm of the crossed arms of Cupid and Psyche and in conveying a very delicate shift from calm to dynamic movement, from force

ANTONIO CANOVA. 1757–1822
CUPID AND PSYCHE (CUPID'S KISS). 1796
Marble. Height 137 cm, length 172 cm

ANTONIO CANOVA. 1757–1822
THE THREE GRACES. 1813–16
Marble. Height 122 cm

96 /97 /98

GIACOMO MANZÙ. 1908–1990
TEBE SEATED. 1983
Bronze

GIORGIO MORANDI. 1890–1964
STILL LIFE
Oil on canvas. 51 x 57.5 cm

GIORGIO MORANDI. 1890–1964
METAPHYSICAL STILL LIFE. 1918
Oil on canvas. 71.5 x 61.5 cm

to weakness. Marble in Canova's works is strikingly picturesque and seems to be now transparent and radiating light and now solid, material and earthly. No less remarkable is Canova's sculptural group *The Three Graces*. The beautiful female bodies are a classical ideal of beauty embodied by the artist in the composition filled with harmony and perfection.

The nineteenth century was the period of a decline in Italian visual arts. The fragmented country fought for its unification almost the whole century and attained its goal only in 1870. A desire to regain a prominent place in European fine arts led to the emergence in the early twentieth century of the first avant-garde trends — Futurism and Metaphysical Painting. The Hermitage's small collection of twentieth-century Italian art was not formed on a regular basis — the works either came from the collections of modern art nationalized after the revolution or were acquired at exhibitions, or were received as gifts. There are, however, few paintings by well-known artists. The gems of the collection are two still lifes by one of the most significant and unusual Italian painters — Giorgio Morandi. The artist painted *Metaphysical Still Life* during the period of his infatuation with the work of Giorgio de Chirico, a predecessor of Surrealism. Chirico created a new metaphysical theory according to which the artist should reflect the world only in terms of imagery that he conjures up from the depth of the subconscious. In Chirico's opinion, "what is profound, is strange, and what is strange is unknown and unexplored." And therefore quite real objects, but casually accumulated, as it were, in Morandi's *Metaphysical Still Life* look strange and enigmatic. In the 1980s the Hermitage held several successful exhibitions of major Italian sculptors and as a sign of gratitude they presented examples of their work to the Hermitage Museum. Thus quite a sizeable collection of Italian sculpture of the second half of the twentieth century was assembled. Its highlights are three bronze statues and reliefs by Giacomo Manzù, one of the leading twentieth-century masters of the realist trend.

THE NETHERLANDS

The Hermitage's collection of Netherlandish art of the fifteenth and sixteenth centuries is comparatively small. In the eighteenth century, when the Hermitage collection was intensely enlarged, the Netherlandish "primitives" were not in demand with collectors and were only occasionally purchased for the museum. Worthy of special note among several works by the Old Netherlandish Masters acquired for the Hermitage during the reign of Catherine the Great was the triptych *The Healing of the Blind Man of Jericho* by Lucas van Leyden, which came from the collection of Pierre Crozat. The major part of the Netherlandish "primitives" appeared in Russia thanks to nineteenth-century art collectors. One of them was the diplomat Dmitry Tatishchev, who bequeathed his collection to the Hermitage in 1845. A gem of Tatishchev's collection was a diptych by Robert Campin, known also as the Master of Flémalle. The large collection of the well-known Russian geographer and traveller Piotr Semionov-Tien-Shansky, which came to the Hermitage in 1915 as his bequest and consisted mostly of Dutch paintings, also included several works by old Netherlandish artists. Little by little the Hermitage accumulated a moderate yet quite valuable collection of Netherlandish painting of the fifteenth and sixteenth centuries. Unfortunately this section suffered greatly in the 1920s: the only work by Jan van Eyck in the museum, *The Annunciation*, was sold by the Soviet government (now it can be found in the National Gallery of Art, Washington). The history of Netherlandish art is inseparably linked with the history of the country. During the Middle Ages the Netherlands, or the Low Countries, the territory lying in the lower reaches of the rivers Rhine, Maas and Scheldt, consisted of a series of separate principalities. In the fourteenth and fifteenth centuries these were united under the Duke of Burgundy and later became part of the Hapsburg Empire. In 1556, when the German Emperor Charles V resigned, the Netherlands became the possession of his son, King Philip II of Spain. A favourable geographical position and an advanced state of crafts and trade promoted the development of Netherlandish cities and towns that led in turn to the flowering of arts in the area. In the fifteenth century the Netherlandish school of painting began to take shape.

Early Netherlandish painting is represented in the Hermitage by Robert Campin, an artist who founded, together with Jan van Eyck, the national school of painting. Like his great contemporary, Campin painted religious subjects. One of his best works is the Hermitage's diptych the wings of which are thematically connected companion pieces. The right-hand one, *The Virgin and Child by a Fireplace* is devoted to Christ's childhood and the left-hand one, *The Holy Trinity*, depicts the dead Christ in the arms of God the Father, with the dove, a symbol of the Holy Ghost, hovering nearby. The flattened, symmetrical composition of *The Trinity* is based on the traditional icon pattern worked

THE SMALL HERMITAGE
ROOM OF NETHERLANDISH ART: 15th and 16th Centuries

out as early as the Middle Ages. Unlike it, the right-hand wing looks absolutely real. The Virgin, depicted as a fair-haired Netherlandish woman with a baby in her hands, is set in the interior of a burgher home with furnishings typical of that time. With care for detail characteristic of Netherlandish artists, Campin thoroughly paints the folds of the Virgin's clothes, highlights the gold of her streaming hair and stresses the strikingly vivid gesture of her arm.

Rogier van der Weyden (Rogelet de la Pâture) was Campin's most celebrated pupil. The Hermitage canvas *St Luke Drawing a Portrait of the Virgin* is known in several versions. The picture is based on a legend that the Evangelist St Luke painted a likeness

99 / 100

NETHERLANDISH MASTER
OF THE 16TH CENTURY
ST JAMES
Wood

ROBERT CAMPIN. *Ca* 1380–1444
THE TRINITY. The left-hand wing
of a diptych
Oil on panel. 34 x 24.5 cm

101 / 102

ROBERT CAMPIN. *Ca* 1380–1444
THE VIRGIN AND CHILD BY A FIREPLACE
The right-hand wing of a diptych
Oil on panel. 34 x 24.5 cm

NETHERLANDISH MASTER
OF THE 16TH CENTURY
ST BARTHOLOMEW
Wood

of the Virgin and Child when he had a vision of them. St Luke was considered to be the patron of artists and the artists' guilds in the Netherlands and Italy were named after him. The composition of this monumental painting is characteristic of Netherlandish art in general: the large figures in the foreground do not obstruct a view of the quiet landscape receding into the depth that can be seen between the columns. Like all famous Netherlandish artists, Rogier van der Weyden perfectly commanded the medium of oil painting which had been evolved in the Netherlands. The artist uses sonorous, saturated colour combinations to convey the texture of silk and brocade, the golden embroidery of clothes, the sparkling of gems and the matt soft skin of the Virgin and Child. The story how the Hermitage became the owner of this painting is quite unusual. When the picture was in a Spanish monastery it had been cut into two parts. The right-hand part with the figure of the Evangelist was acquired for the Hermitage at the sale of the collection of William II of the Netherlands. Later, in 1884, a Parisian dealer brought to St Petersburg and

103 / 104

ROGIER VAN DER WEYDEN. *Ca* 1400–1464
ST LUKE DRAWING A PORTRAIT OF THE VIRGIN
Oil on canvas, transferred from a panel
102.5 x 108.5 cm

ASCRIBED TO HUGO VAN DER GOES
THE LAMENTATION
Oil on panel. 36.2 x 30.2 cm

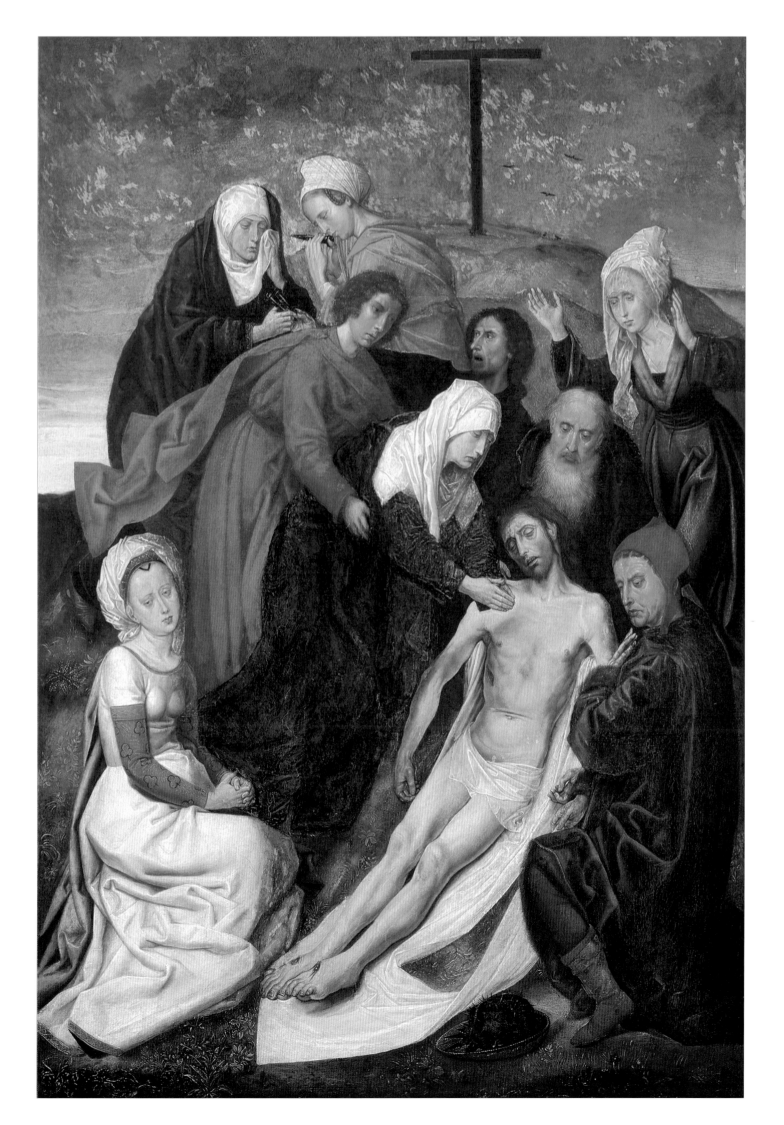

105 / 106

MASTER OF THE FEMALE HALF-LENGTHS
Active in Antwerp in the 1530s and 1540s
MUSICIANS
Oil on panel. 53 x 37.5 cm

DIRCK JACOBSZ. *Ca* 1497–1567
**GROUP PORTRAIT OF THE CORPORATION
OF AMSTERDAM SHOOTERS.** 1532
Oil on canvas, transferred from a panel
115 x 160 cm

sold to the museum a representation of the Virgin which has turned out to be, as shown by research, the left-hand part of Rogier's picture. The Hermitage specialists reunited the two parts of the composition. This is how the Virgin "appeared" to St Luke a second time.

Hugo van der Goes, who was active in Gent, belonged to the next generation of major Netherlandish artists. The Hermitage owns two works ascribed to him: the large altar triptych *The Adoration of the Magi* and the small painting *The Lamentation over the Dead Christ*, an almost exact replica of the right-hand wing of Goes's diptych now in the Kunsthistorisches Museum, Vienna. *The Lamentation* is filled with a profound sorrow and intense drama. The artist shows Mary Magdalene stiffed in despair by the feet of Christ, Joseph looks austere and restrained, and the Virgin tenderly touches the shoulder of Her Son. The figures in the background express their emotions in a more vivid way: Mary, sister of Lazarus, has raised her arms to heavens; St John is supporting the Virgin and his posture suggests that he shares her grief. The gloomy hill of Calvary soars over the Lamentation scene with a lonely cross against the dismal, stormy skies as a symbol of the tragedy.

In the sixteenth century, as the result of its close ties with Italy and the spread of the ideas of Humanism, Netherlandish art, while retaining its distinctive features, underwent important changes: there emerge new genres and works on traditional Christian themes began to acquire an increasingly secular character. The first decades of the sixteenth century saw the emergence in the Netherlands of a new movement, Romanism, based on an imitation of Italian examples. Adherents of this movement introduced nudes into their mythological subjects. Paintings with overtly secular subjects began to appear gaining enormous popularity in the aristocratic circles

of Netherlandish society. Beautiful examples of such painting are elegant, graceful female images created by an unknown artist, the Master of the Female Half-Lengths, who was active in Antwerp in the 1530s and 1540s.

A place apart in sixteenth-century painting is occupied by the group portrait. This kind of portraiture was widespread later — in Dutch and Flemish painting of the seventeenth century. Such portraits were usually commissioned for the decoration of the interiors of city halls where they, as a rule, can be found today. They are quite rare beyond the borders of the Netherlands. The *Group Portrait of the Corporation of Amsterdam Shooters* by Dirck Jakobs is an early example of works of this type. The first half of the sixteenth century was the period when

the celebrated Pieter Bruegel the Elder and Lucas van Leyden created their works. Lucas van Leyden is represented in the Hermitage by one of his most remarkable works, the triptych *The Healing of the Blind Man of Jericho*. Although the tryptich is devoted to the well-known biblical subject, it has little in common with religious compositions of the previous period. Lucas van Leyden's work is neither

107

LUCAS VAN LEYDEN. 1489/94–1533
THE HEALING OF THE BLIND MAN OF JERICHO. 1531
Triptych. Oil on canvas, transferred from a panel. 115.5 x 150.5 cm; 89 x 33.5 cm

pervaded with a deep pious mood nor has a majestic atmosphere. The artist treats the subject as a genre scene. The painting was perhaps intended for the Leyden military hospital rather than for a cathedral altar and so the artist focuses on the edifying aspect of the Gospel subject. On the side wings of the triptych the artist placed, instead of traditional images of saints, distinctly secular figures of a warrior and a girl demonstrating coats-of-arms of the commissioners — the Leyden burgher Jacob Floriszon van Monfort and his wife.

We can have some idea about the work of the great Pieter Bruegel (between 1525 and 1530–1569) from works by his son, Pieter Brueghel the Younger, who often copied his father's paintings. The Gospel subject of *The Adoration of the Magi* is set on winter streets of a Netherlandish town, crowded with people engaged in their daily occupations. The procession of the Magi, who are going to greet the Infant Christ, seem to be dissolved in the flow of this life spiritualized by Brueghel's specific style, in which all phenomena are pervaded with timeless, sacred meaning. In the second half of the sixteenth century Netherlandish painting gradually lost its ties with the best traditions of the precious period. Towards the

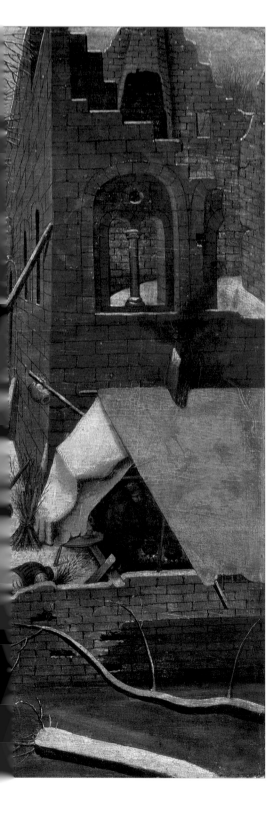

PIETER BRUEGHEL THE YOUNGER. *Ca* 1564–1638
THE ADORATION OF THE MAGI
Oil on canvas. 36 x 56 cm

GIJSBRECHT LIJTENS (?). 1586 – after 1643
WINTER LANDSCAPE
Oil on panel. 71.5 x 89 cm

end of the century only landscape painting retained its popularity. Painters specialized in definite types of landscape scenes — some of them painted mountains and forests, some others depicted villages, towns and cities, and still others portrayed different seasons. At the turn of the sixteenth and seventeenth centuries, when the Netherlands in fact ceased to exist as a single state, there began the formation of two independent schools — the Dutch School in the north and the Flemish in the south. However, for a long time in both parts of the Netherlandish states there were artists who combined in their work the traditions of old Netherlandish art and innovative quests. One of them was the anonymous painter active in the Netherlands at the beginning of the seventeenth century and conventionally called the Master of Winter Landscapes. Some researches identify him as the Antwerp landscape painter Gijsbrecht Lijtens. The *Winter Landscape* owned by the Hermitage features an elaborate pattern of the naked branches of powerful trees filling the light, almost monochrome space of the picture with a low horizon. The artist was apparently interested in the possibility to convey the interrelationships of light, colour and air medium — the feature that would become a specific quality of Dutch painting in the seventeenth century. The artist who stood on the threshold of innovative discoveries in the field of landscape painting in the seventeenth century was the younger brother of Pieter Brueghel the Elder — Jan, who was nicknamed the Velvet Brueghel. The artist's nickname emphasizes the specific aspect of his work appreciated by his contemporaries. Jan Brueghel received this nickname largely for his predilection to rich clothes, but another reason was a special velvety quality and softness of his artistic manner. His small-scale landscapes were striking for their virtuoso blend of diverse, subtly developed, sonorous greenish and bluish tints. Like fifteenth-century Netherlandish masters, Jan Brueghel used only pure, resonant colours in his palette evading black and mixed monochrome shades. The harmonious and beautiful art of the Velvet Brueghel, which covers the turn of the two centuries, completed the great age of the Netherlandish Renaissance.

FRANCE

The Hermitage's world-famous French collection that is deservedly considered the pride of the museum contains many masterpieces of painting, sculpture and applied art of the fifteenth to twentieth century. It fills more than fifty rooms of the Winter Palace and represents practically all the styles and trends of French art. Works by nearly every major French artist can be found in it. There is no collection outside France capable to rival the Hermitage in the quantity and quality of superb examples of French painting, sculpture and decorative art. Many of the masterpieces dating from the seventeenth and eighteenth centuries were acquired by Catherine the Great, known as an ardent admirer of French style and fashion. Among the connoisseurs and professionals who advised the Russian Empress on artistic matters were the famous French Enlighteners Denis Diderot and Melchior Grimm. Diderot promoted Catherine's acquisition of the most prominent works by contemporary masters who won recognition at official exhibitions in Paris. As a result the Hermitage came to possess some of the best canvases by leading eighteenth-century artists. The earliest Hermitage works of French art date from the Middle Ages. The excellent collection of Alexander Bazilewsky, which was acquired in 1885, yielded several superb examples of French applied art of this period created mainly between the eleventh and thirteenth centuries: church silverware adorned with gems, ivory statuettes of the Madonna, caskets and folding icons embellished with varicoloured enamels. The twelfth century is represented in the Hermitage collection by a masterpiece of French applied art — a reliquary made in the shape of

St Etienne, a very rare example of the Romanesque style. Despite an abundance of details, a small wooden statue, covered with leaf gold and embellished with gems, has a generalized and monumental appearance. In the thirteenth century Paris became the main centre of ivory carving that was a popular medieval craft. The cult of the Madonna characteristic of the Catholic countries led to the creation of numerous subtly coloured ivory statuettes. Muffled in long and wide, freely falling cloaks, the statuettes of the Madonna usually stood in home chapels. The famous Hermitage's collection of Limoges enamels gives a full idea of the basic phases in the development of this handicraft in France. As early as the twelfth century Limoges was well known for its workshops involved in the decoration of metal objects with champlevé enamels — a process during which a vitrified alloy of various colours was poured into hollows made on the metal surface and then fired. The Hermitage collection of Limoges articles dating from the fifteenth and sixteenth centuries and including three-wing altarpieces, dishes and bowls, as well as some secular items demonstrates the then new technique of enamel painting. According to this new method enamel colours were applied in layers on a copper or bronze plaque and fired several times. In fact, the Limoges enamels paintings allow us

THE WINTER PALACE
ROOM OF FRENCH ART: 18th Century

110 / 111 / 112 / 113

MASTER OF THE THUISON ALTARPIECE
15th century
THE ENTRY INTO JERUSALEM
Oil on panel. 116.5 x 51.5 cm

THE VIRGIN AND CHILD. Late 13th century
Ivory. Height 22.5 cm

RELIQUARY: *ST ETIENNE.* Late 12th century
Wood, silver, coloured stones. Height 42.5 cm

THE ADORATION OF THE MAGI
Central part of a three-winged icon
Early 16th century. Limoges, France
Enamel colours

to have an idea of fifteenth-century French painting as a whole. Works by French painters from this period outside France are extremely rare. This makes even more valuable the bright-coloured wing of an altarpiece, *The Entry into Jerusalem*. It is attributed to the so-called Master of the Thuison Altarpiece who was active in Amiens and received his name after his only known work.

The flowering of the Renaissance in France began in the sixteenth century, later than in some other European countries. French culture, which found itself between two major centres of the Renaissance, the Netherlands and Germany in the north and Italy in the south, took the favour of its position assimilating the best accomplishments of these countries and evolving a distinctive national style of its own. The wide-scale activities of the French court and primarily the efforts of King Françis I, the last representative of the Valois dynasty, played a major role in the brilliant flourishing of Renaissance culture. This educated monarch, an enthusiastic admirer of Classical Antiquity and Italian Renaissance, accumulated rich art collections in his new residence at Fontainebleau. Françis I assembled at his court a whole team of the best French painters, sculptors and craftsmen and invited a number of celebrities from Italy. Even the great Leonardo da Vinci spent his last

117

years in France. It is largely due to the Italian artists active at Fontainebleau that the French Renaissance developed its elegant aristocratic style.

The excellent Hermitage collection of French portraiture enables us to form a good notion of refined French Renaissance culture which combined aristocratic purity of style with a love for individual and characteristic features. This period saw superb achievements in the field of pencil portraiture — large-scale drawings skilfully executed in free, light strokes and tinted with sanguine, chalks, charcoal or pastel. Usually such drawings were commissioned as independent works in their own right. Pierre Dumonstier was an outstanding master of pencil portraiture and a representative of the well-known dynasty of artists. All the seven signed sheets by this master, among which the portrait of his brother Etienne Dumonstier, court painter to Catherine de' Medici, is worthy of particular notice, are superb examples of the elegant French style. The only specimen of Renaissance sculpture — the marble relief *Venus and Cupid* attributed to the celebrated French sculptor Jean Goujon, gives an idea of this kind of art that was very popular in France in the sixteenth century. Goujon, close to the Fontainebleau school, pervaded his composition with elaborate, flowing rhythms characteristic of masters of this trend and filled them with graceful figures of elongated pro-

portions. The flowering of French culture in the seventeenth century started its triumph all over Europe. The art of this period is well represented in the Hermitage collection. A desire to capture the real world can be observed in intimate works by the three Le Nain brothers. The most talented of them, Louis Le Nain, is represented in the Hermitage by two paintings — the world-famous *The Milkwoman's Family* and an earlier canvas, *A Visit to Grandmother*. The subject of *The Milkwoman's Family*, a painting classed with the so-called "peasant genre", is, however, devoid of any everyday narrative details or entertaining features. The figures of French peasants, shown immobile against the background of the immense, grey-bluish sky, together with a donkey — an indispensable member of a rural family in those times — are full of epic grandeur. The restrained light colour scheme seems to be monochrome at first sight, but an attentive eye will discern hundreds of warm brownish and yellow shades harmonizing with

PIERRE DUMONSTIER. *Ca* 1540 – after 1600
PORTRAIT OF A YOUTH
Oil on canvas. 32 x 19 cm

JEAN GOUJON (?). 1510–1568
VENUS AND CUPID
Marble. 51 x 57 cm

LOUIS LE NAIN. 1593–1648
THE DAIRYWOMAN'S FAMILY. 1640s
Oil on canvas. 51 x 59 cm

the cold blue and grey hues predominant in the chromatic range of the painting. The strictly balanced and thought-out composition of this unassuming genre scene is typical of the best examples of French Classicism, the elevated style of art evolved by the great Poussin in the seventeenth century. The work of Nicolas Poussin is represented in the Hermitage Museum by twelve paintings revealing the essence of his painterly system on which he worked in the course of many years. The blend of reasonable clarity and profound lyrical feeling interpreted by the artist as a heroic feat, the truly musical harmony of linear rhythms and colour spots, the lofty beauty of the characters — all these features distinguish the painting *Tancred and Erminia*, a masterpieces in the Poussin collection. The picture is based on a subject borrowed from *Jerusalem Delivered*, a poem by the Italian Renaissance poet Torquato Tasso. At the end of the 1640s Poussin created a series of majestic and beautiful landscapes devoted to the harmonious unity of eternal Nature and all creatures inhabiting it. The earth, trees, mountains, gods, people, nymphs and satyrs in the landscape with Polythemus seem to listen, holding their breath, to the magic sounds of the pipe played by the Cyclops Polythemus who suffers from his unrequited love to the nymph Galatea.

Seventeenth-century France, the classical country of an absolute European monarchy, witnessed the birth of a "grand style" which largely determined specific features in the development of French architecture, sculpture, painting and even applied art throughout almost the entire century. Nevertheless, French art of this period shows a striking variety of styles and creative individualities. Simon Vouet, court painter to Louis XIII, expressed all the peculiar traits of the "grand style" in his typical formal painting — the *Allegorical Portrait of Queen Anne of Austria as Minerva*. The large size of this canvas, its monumental composition and bright local colours are meant for the perception of the picture from a large distance.

The Hermitage collection of French art of the eighteenth century has no equals elsewhere in the world. All the leading masters of painting, sculpture and decorative arts of the "gallant" century are amply represented

117

NICOLAS POUSSIN. 1594–1665
**LANDSCAPE
WITH POLYTHEMUS.** 1649
Oil on canvas. 150 x 199 cm

118 / 119

NICOLAS POUSSIN. 1594–1665
TANCRED AND ERMINIA. 1630s
Oil on canvas. 98.5 x 146.5 cm

SIMON VOUET. 1590–1649
**ALLEGORICAL PORTRAIT OF QUEEN ANNE
OF AUSTRIA AS MINERVA.** *Ca* 1643
Oil on canvas. 202 x 172 cm

in the Hermitage. Masterpieces by Watteau, Boucher, Chardin, Fragonard and Greuze, outstanding pieces of sculpture by Falconet and Houdon allow visitors to familiarize themselves with the French fine arts of the eighteenth century as a whole. Antoine Watteau is recognized as a seminal figure of the style that determined the character of French culture in the eighteenth century — the virtuoso and artistic Rococo. Watteau introduced a special kind of festive scenes, so called *fêtes galantes*, in which elegant and gracious characters performed, with a tinge of irony, scenes from a spectacle about mysterious and intriguing relations between men and women. However, with all the resplendence and seeming ease of the gallant style of this "darling of fortune" and idol of the French aristocracy, Watteau's paintings are elaborate and meaningful. The artist himself rarely named his works, and their subjects defy description in words. Usually their names were suggested by somebody in the artist's entourage. Indeed, we may only surmise what could happen between elegant ladies and exquisite cavaliers in the scene unfolding before us in *An Embarrassing Proposal*. This scene, both theatrical and deeply natural, is almost devoid of outward action, yet one cannot fail to sense its profound emotional undertones. The young girls and cavaliers in gaily coloured, elegant garments seem to be separated from spectators by a transparent wall; their fragile, exquisite and somewhat sorrowful realm

120 / 121 / 122

ANTOINE WATTEAU. 1684–1721
THE CAPRICIOUS WOMAN. *Ca* 1718
Oil on canvas. 42 x 34 cm

FRANÇOIS BOUCHER. 1703–1770
THE TOILET OF VENUS
Oil on canvas. 101 x 86.7 cm (oval)

ANTOINE WATTEAU. 1684–1721
AN EMBARRASSING PROPOSAL. *Ca* 1716
Oil on canvas. 65 x 84.5 cm

SERVICE WITH CAMEOS. 1778–79
The Sèvres Porcelain Factory

THE "LARGE" CARRIAGE
First quarter of the 18th century
The Gobelins Factory, France (?)

is inaccessible as a beautiful dream. *The Capricious Woman* is generally recognized as one of Watteau's masterpieces. The gallant scene of a "siege" undertaken by a cavalier, experienced in the game of love, for the seduction of a young beauty, charming, proud and capricious, is transformed by Watteau into a pageant of colour and light based on subtle shades and half-tones. Artists of the so-called "Watteau school" merely used his outward technical devices that became the basis of the Rococo style. The festive and lively spirit of this style is embodied best of all in the works of François Boucher. He rendered with equal ease and dexterity a pastoral or mythological scene, a landscape or a portrait, and had no problems with designing a stage set, a costume, a tapestry or a porcelain piece. The most fashionable artist of his time, Boucher had the title of the first painter to the King. He was also Director of the Royal Tapestry Factory and President of the Academy of Arts. His paintings perfectly matched the interiors of elegant eighteenth-century palaces making up a beautiful single whole with furniture, decorative sculpture and tapestries. Boucher never sought to convey deep feelings and subtle sensations. His rich fantasy combined with a somewhat ironic and frivolous approach to the world brings forth a great number of light-minded and

smart shepherds and shepherdesses, ancient gods and goddesses, nonchalantly flirting against a background of no less beautiful and artificial scenery. Boucher's light, pinkish-blue colours are pleasant to the eye, his drawing is whimsical and elegant. Two Hermitage's

125 / 126 / 127

WATCH ON CHÂTELAINE. 1740s–1750s
Paris. By Pierre Le Roy
Gold, silver, glass, enamel, metal alloys, diamonds, rubies. Length of châtelaine 18.6 cm; diameter of clock 4.7 cm

WATCH ON CHÂTELAINE WITH ENAMEL DIAL
Late 1770s – early 1780s
St Petersburg. By Jean Fazy
Gold, silver, brilliants, rose-cut diamonds, enamel, glass, emeralds, chased and gilloché. Length of châtelaine 13 cm; diameter of clock 4.2 cm

BACK OF A STATE BEDSTEAD
Second half of the 17th century. Detail
Embroidery on gold thread and coloured silk
200 x 128 cm

companion paintings inscribed into the then fashionable oval form and devoted to the goddess of love — *The Toilet of Venus* and *The Triumph of Venus* — demonstrate Boucher at his best. The ancient goddess of beauty was one of the most popular subjects in Rococo art, but the appearance of Boucher's heroine is far from classical ancient canons. Boucher as a painter asserted the ideal of female beauty of his time. The elegant, not tall, snub-nosed blonde with a plump body embodied the truly French grace, sensuality, careless lightness and became a symbol of the entire Rococo period.

The Rococo style most vividly revealed itself in numerous examples of decorative art. All that encircles man — furniture, carriages, fabrics, vessels and bronze — seem to radiate a light, frivolous mood created by bright colours and whimsical arabesques (the term 'rococo' is commonly derived from a French word *rocaille* or shell). A fine example of the Rococo style is the Hermitage's "Large" Carriage. Peter the Great acquired it at the Gobelins Royal Factory in Paris during his second travel abroad in 1716–17. The carriage, glistening with gold and richly adorned with velvet, was intended solely for coronation ceremonies held in the Assumption Cathedral in Moscow. The Hermitage owns one of the largest collections of French eighteenth-century tapestries — woven carpets produced mainly at the Gobelins Royal Factory. These superb decorative compositions, noted for their hand-worked pictorial designs based on sketches by notable painters and woven in wool with an addition of golden and silver thread, became known as Gobelins after the family which had established the tapestry factory.

The second half of the eighteenth century saw an unusual flourishing of the art of porcelain in France. The discovery of kaolin deposits in 1768 made it possible to manufacture real, "hard" porcelain. Even the earliest examples of articles produced at the

128 / 129 / 130

JEAN-BAPTISTE SIMÉON CHARDIN. 1699–1779
GRACE BEFORE MEAT. 1744
Oil on canvas. 49.5 x 38.4 cm

JEAN-BAPTISTE SIMÉON CHARDIN. 1699–1779
THE WASHERWOMAN
Oil on canvas. 37.5 x 42.7 cm

JEAN-BAPTISTE SIMÉON CHARDIN. 1699–1779
STILL LIFE WITH ATTRIBUTES OF THE ARTS. 1766
Oil on canvas. 112 x 140.5 cm

Sèvres Factory were notable for their high quality, elegant forms and bright colours (green, blue, pink and yellow) retaining their freshness after firing. The Hermitage's porcelain services manufactured at Sèvres demonstrate the best qualities of this kind of decorative art. But the Service with Cameos produced for Catherine the Great in 1778–79 stands out even among these fine items for its elegance. Intended for sixty diners and including more than seven hundred pieces, it strikes us by the perfection of its forms and the excellence of its decor. The whiteness of thin porcelain and its gilt decoration highlight the bright blue tone, happily found by the designers. The refined floral ornament is embellished with painted insets imitating ancient cameos.

An appeal to reason combined with an interest in natural, healthy and harmonious life became the main spiritual criteria of the age of Enlightenment — a brief yet remarkable period in French culture of the second half of the eighteenth century. The work of Jean-Baptiste Siméon Chardin developed along the lines of philosophical and aesthetic ideals of the great French Encyclopedists Voltaire, Diderot, Rousseau and Montesquieu. The Hermitage paintings

by Chardin brilliantly demonstrate his skill to make emphasis in common everyday scenes on spiritual, harmonious and poetic qualities. Chardin began his career as a painter of still lifes. Before him still-life painting was considered the lowest form in French art. But Chardin treated still life not merely as a *nature morte*, an assemblage of "dead" objects. Objects depicted by Chardin have a soul; they live an independent life of their own. *The Washerwoman* and *Grace before Meat* rank with Chardin's most famous everyday scenes which he began to paint already after having won renown as a still-life painter. Both pictures convincingly represent a peaceful, unhurried pace of life of the third-estate people to which the artist himself belonged. These modest intimate works pervaded with a striking harmony and poetic mood are truly beautiful. The rival of Watteau himself in the elegance of his palette, Chardin applies colours on to canvas in small, but very thick divided strokes reminiscent of mosaics. This technique that seems to be nearly impressionistic at a close range, amazes viewers at a distance by an illusion of palpable details and a wealth of shades of light and colour. The Hermitage possesses one of the best collections of eighteenth-century French easel sculpture. It includes several works by Etienne-Maurice Falconet. Almost all of his pieces in the Hermitage collections had been produced by Falconet in Paris and brought by himself to Russia. The French sculptor was invited by Catherine the Great to St Petersburg for the creation of a monument to Peter the Great (this work became famous as *The Bronze Horseman*). Falconet's works in the Hermitage give an idea of his widest creative scope — the sculptor began his artistic career during the refined Rococo age, imbibed the dramatic expressiveness of the Baroque and assimilated the perfect poise of Classicism. *Cupid Menacing with His Finger* is one of the most popular statues of the Rococo period known in numerous replicas.

The brilliant work of Jean Honoré Fragonard was the last outburst of departing Rococo art at the end of the eighteenth century, on the eve of great transformations awaiting French society. Fragonard's creative range was extremely wide. The artist was equally skilled in various painterly techniques. *The Lost Forfeit, or the Captured Kiss* with its free sketchy manner is close to a masterfully executed study. *The Snatched Kiss*, remarkable for a picturesque character of the scene, a thorough treatment of details and a careful rendering of the texture of materials, recalls masterpieces of painting by the Small Dutch Masters. The sharpness of

131 / 132 / 133

JEAN HONORÉ FRAGONARD. 1732–1806
THE SNATCHED KISS. Late 1780s
Oil on canvas. 45 x 55 cm

JEAN HONORÉ FRAGONARD. 1732–1806
THE LOST FORFEIT, OR THE CAPTURED KISS
Oil on canvas. 47 x 60 cm

ETIENNE MAURICE FALCONET. 1716–1791
**CUPID MENACING WITH
HIS FINGER.** 1758
Marble. Height 85 cm

the scene seemingly spied in a casual manner endows the canvas with a distinctly French charm. Art of the first half of the nineteenth century is represented in the Hermitage by canvases of major French artists. Their works reflect a complex and dramatic struggle of ideas and movements characteristic of this period. Paintings by David, Gérard, Gros and Ingres demonstrate the basic principles of Neo-Classicism — the artistic trend which was born on the eve of the French Revolution. Its leading figure was Jacques Louis David. The artist created *Sappho and Phaon* already during the period of the First Empire when he became court painter to the new French Emperor, Napoleon Bonaparte. Tired of bloody revolutionary events, society needed new, lyrical heroes and artists found them in ancient myths and legends. The image of Sappho, a famous ancient Greek poetess, was a recurrent motif with Neo-Classicist artists. She fell in love with the young beautiful Phaon being not young and committed suicide unable to bear the torments of unrequited love. Even more popular with artists of this period was Napoleon. In the eyes of the ardent and romantic Jean Antoine Gros the exploits of the army leader, the future Emperor of France, were on a par with the glorious deeds of ancient heroes. In his painting *Napoleon Bonaparte on the Arcole Bridge* David's favourite pupil depicted a real feat showing the young French commander's courage that proved to be decisive

for the outcome of the Battle of Arcole on 15–17 November 1796. The talent of Jean Auguste Dominique Ingres, the most significant figure in David's circle, was revealed during the years of the First Empire. Ingres showed himself a true innovator in portraiture. His only work in the Hermitage, *Portrait of Count Nikolai Guryev*, may be considered one of the best examples of this kind of painting. The precise, expressive drawing and restrained noble colour range in combination with the thorough modelling of form lend a truly classical completeness to this work. At the same time the portrait is remarkable for the complexity and depth of the model's psychological delineation. The canvas

134 / 135 / 136 / 137

JACQUES LOUIS DAVID. 1748–1825
SAPPHO AND PHAON. 1809
Oil on canvas. 225.3 x 262 cm

ANTOINE JEAN GROS. 1771–1835
NAPOLEON BONAPARTE ON THE ARCOLE BRIDGE
Replica of the painting produced in 1797
Oil on canvas. 134 x 104 cm

EUGÈNE DELACROIX. 1798–1863
LION HUNT IN MOROCCO. 1854
Oil on canvas. 74 x 92 cm

JEAN AUGUSTE DOMINIQUE INGRES. 1780–1867
PORTRAIT OF COUNT NIKOLAI GURYEV. 1821
Oil on canvas. 107 x 86 cm

138 / 139 / 140

CLAUDE OSCAR MONET. 1840–1926
LADY IN THE GARDEN AT SAINTE-ADRESSE. 1867
Oil on canvas. 80 x 99 cm

CLAUDE OSCAR MONET. 1840–1926
CORNER OF THE GARDEN AT MONTGERON. 1876–77
Oil on canvas. 172 x 193 cm

CLAUDE OSCAR MONET. 1840–1926
THE POND AT MONTGERON. 1876–77
Oil on canvas. 173 x 193 cm

captured the troubled state of the sitter's soul concealed behind Count Guryev's outward restraint. This quality of Ingres's portrait foretells the discoveries of the Romantic school, which declared the arrival of a new artistic movement ready to replace Neo-Classicism in the early 1820s. Eugène Delacroix, the greatest of French Romantic artists, is represented in the Hermitage by two small paintings from the later phase of his work. The themes of mysterious East, fascinating for a European's imagination, occupied a prominent place in Romantic art. Delacroix had made a journey to Algeria and Morocco as early as 1832, but even twenty years later his Moroccan impressions still inspired ingenious and powerful paintings. His *Lion Hunt in Morocco* is pervaded with energy and dynamism. Delacroix chooses not the culmination of the event but the moment preceding it when tension reaches its peak. He always strove to capture man's forceful emotional thrust expressed in movement. His idea that "the expression of move-ment is more important than the finish of some hand or foot" could be used later by innovative artists who revered Delacroix as one of their spiritual teachers.

132

The turn of the 1860s and 1870s witnessed a deep split between innovators and official artists of the Parisian Salon on the French art scene. In 1874, a group of young artists, not recognized by official criticism and repudiated by the Salon, decided to arrange their own exhibition. The leaders of the group were Claude Monet, Auguste Renoir, Alfred Sisley and Camille Pissarro. The exhibition they arranged caused a scandal and derision in society. It was then that the word "Impressionism" was derived from Monet's painting *Impression, Sunrise* — a derogatory name that would later become the generally accepted title of this new trend in French art. Eight beautiful Hermitage paintings by Monet — from his early *Lady in the Garden* to *Waterloo Bridge*, produced already at the beginning of the next, twentieth century, illustrate the evolution of his creative manner. Working mainly out of doors, Monet aimed to capture the changeable character of weather, a wealth of colouristic shades ever changing under the impact of light and air, softening the outlines of volumes and reducing them to a picturesque spot. These efforts led him to the use of a special sweeping, sketchy manner of painting. Seeking to convey as precisely as possible inimitable fleeting moments, Monet and his friends usually turned to small-scale canvases. Even two monumental works, *The Pond at Montgeron* and *Corner of the Garden at Montgeron* were executed according to the principle of an immediate sketch from nature. Monet could enjoy for hours their fleeting beauty recording in dashing brushstrokes ever new pictorial harmonies emerging under the impact of changing illumination. Such method of work often led him to create a series of several paintings treating the same motif in a different colour scheme. The Hermitage's haystack at Giverny belongs to one of such series, which is a perfect example of Monet's Impressionist manner. Separate pure dabs of yellow, green and red colour shades, mixed in the viewer's eye rather than on the palette, bring forth a sense

141

CAMILLE PISSARRO. 1830–1903
**PLACE DU THÉÂTRE-FRANÇAIS
IN PARIS.** 1898
Oil on canvas. 65.5 x 81.5 cm

142 / 143

CAMILLE PISSARRO. 1830–1903
BOULEVARD MONTMARTRE IN PARIS. 1897
Oil on canvas. 73 x 92 cm

ALFRED SISLEY. 1839–1899
VILLENEUVE-LA-GARENNE. 1872
Oil on canvas. 59 x 80.5 cm

of a beautiful painted pageant that the Impressionists could observe in any, even most common detail of the real world.

Following Delacroix's statement that "grey is the enemy of any painting", Monet and his friends, the landscape painters Alfred Sisley and Camille Pissarro, expelled indefinite grey shades as well as black and white tints from their palette, because as they said, they "did not see them in living nature". Alfred Sisley, who was endowed with an unusually subtle colouristic gift, liked to paint picturesque environs of Paris on the spot. His canvases permeated with light seem to be more traditional and quiet in comparison with temperamental and dynamic landscape by Monet. Sisley's *Village on the Seine, Villeneuve-la-Garenne* is undoubtedly one of the most lyrical works of early Impressionism.

Camille Pissarro's favourite subject was Paris, which he painted during all seasons. The city invariably looks vivid and festive, changing and

144 / 145 / 146

PIERRE AUGUSTE RENOIR. 1841–1919
CHILD WITH A WHIP. 1885
Oil on canvas. 105 x 75 cm

PIERRE AUGUSTE RENOIR. 1841–1919
GIRL WITH A FAN. 1881
Oil on canvas. 65 x 50 cm

PIERRE AUGUSTE RENOIR. 1841–1919
PORTRAIT OF THE ACTRESS JEANNE SAMARY. 1878
Oil on canvas. 173 x 103 cm

full of unceasing motion in his canvases. Pissarro painted his series of thirteen canvases devoted to Boulevard Montmartre from the window of his studio. The street, crowded with people and carriages, lit by warm sunlight or immersed in a bluish twilight or silvery under the rain, seems to be ever changing. The Hermitage painting *Boulevard Montmartre in Paris* almost tangibly renders a sense of humid air, pervaded with rain, which radiates with a thousand of pearly shades.

The work of Auguste Renoir is one of the brightest and most expressive achievements of French painting in the nineteenth century. Renoir felt at ease handling the complex colours of his canvases, tinged with various shades. The striking chromatic harmonies built on the correlation of warm and cold hues of red and green, blue and orange, yellow and violet were not Renoir's invention — he found them in nature. Renoir worked mainly in the fields of portraiture and nude. The six paintings in the Hermitage collection demonstrate the best qualities of his art. The "beautiful Alphoncine", a charming daughter of *père* Fournaise, the owner of a famous tavern, turns under the painter's brush into a somewhat mysterious *Girl with a Fan*. The radiating greenish background of the picture harmonizes well with the reddish shades of her dress and the armchair upholstery. The girl's dark hair, her eyes and huge bow are saturated with deep and diverse shades of blue. In this lively colour stream the artist's brush captures his characters at the moments of their authentic life. The models posing for Renoir possessed some features in common allowing us to speak about a certain poetic generalization, a sort of "Renoir's" type of woman or child. Renoir was not much concerned with the verisimilitude or psychological characterization of his commissioner, although as a true portrait painter he succeeded in attaining both likelihood and psychological insight. A human face and figure are for the artist primarily a wealth of pictorial relationships. Renoir's painting *Child with a Whip* may be regarded as a typical example of his Impressionism. The artist's protagonist in this painting is sunlight. It seems to dissolve the boy's figure in his environment and to colour his white dress and

the sandy path with greenish, yellow and bluish tints. In his *Portrait of the Actress Jeanne
Samary* Renoir seems to have arrested a beautiful moment. The charming young actress of
the Comédie-Française is shown standing still
in a typical pose of classical formal portraiture. But it seems that she would soon un-
fold her arms and disappear with her enchant-
ing smile leaving behind only a memory of
her wonderful blue eyes, white skin and a
wealth of pictorial hues of her pinkish silk
dress. The manycoloured dense semidarkness
of the background, filled with details of a luxurious interior characteristic of the 1870s, emphasizes the lightness of Jeanne's elegant figure and the bright golden spot of her red hair.

147 / 148 / 149

EDGAR DEGAS. 1834–1917
AFTER THE BATH
Pastel, gouache and tempera on canvas. 82.5 x 72 cm

EDGAR DEGAS. 1834–1917
WOMAN COMBING HER HAIR. *Ca* 1885–86
Pastel on paper. 53 x 52 cm

AUGUSTE RODIN. 1840–1917
ETERNAL SPRING. 1905
Marble. Height 77 cm

150 / 151

PAUL CÉZANNE. 1839–1906
MOUNT SAINTE-VICTOIRE. 1900
Oil on canvas. 78 x 99 cm

PAUL CÉZANNE. 1839–1906
STILL LIFE WITH CURTAIN. *Ca* 1899
Oil on canvas. 53 x 72 cm

152

PAUL CÉZANNE. 1839–1906
LADY IN BLUE. *Ca* 1899
Oil on canvas. 88.5 x 72 cm

"What a marvellous girl," the artist said recalling Jeanne Samary. "And what a skin! It was positively radiating light."

The art of Edgar Degas occupies a special place in the Impressionist movement. Although Degas took part in all Impressionist exhibitions, his work cannot be entirely associated with this artistic trend. The work of this great artist is represented in the Hermitage by a series of large pastels. Degas is considered an unsurpassed master of this difficult medium. His pastels are characterized by rare vivacity and expressiveness of an immediate sketch from nature and at the same time they are thought-out works, calculated to the last detail in composition and linear design and devoid of anything casual. Nudes depicted by Degas do not possess classical proportions and the secret of their beauty lies in the natural character of their movements.

The creative quests of the great French sculptor Auguste Rodin make him largely close to Impressionism. His manner is marked by dynamism, plasticity and emotional tension. Light sliding over the rough surface of marble or bronze dissolves the outlines making his modelling of the shapes nearly as soft as in painting. Rodin's famous marble compositions suggest the changeable state of the world with no less intensity than paintings by Monet or Renoir. In his sculptural group *Eternal Spring* the beautiful bodies of embracing lovers epitomize the eternal feeling of love, the culmination of emotional life.

Paul Cézanne took part in the first exhibition of the Impressionists held in 1874, but unlike Monet, Pissarro and Sisley he did not sought to convey only direct natural impressions. As the artist himself declared, he wanted "to make of Impressionism something solid and durable, like the art of the Museums". The work of Cézanne opens a new phenomenon in the history of French painting — Post-Impressionism. The Hermitage collection of the great painter consists of eleven works exhaustively representing all the phases in the

153 / 154

VINCENT VAN GOGH. 1853–1890
LADIES OF ARLES. 1888
Oil on canvas. 73.5 x 92.5 cm

VINCENT VAN GOGH. 1853–1890
COTTAGES. 1890
Oil on canvas. 60 x 73 cm

155

VINCENT VAN GOGH. 1853–1890
LILAC BUSH. 1889
Oil on canvas. 72 x 92 cm

156 / 157

PAUL GAUGUIN. 1848–1903
NAVE NAVE MOE. **SACRED SPRING
(SWEET DREAMS).** 1894
Oil on canvas. 73 x 98 cm

PAUL GAUGUIN. 1848–1903
PASTORALES TAHITIENNES. 1893
Oil on canvas. 86 x 113 cm

158

PAUL GAUGUIN. 1848–1903
EU HAERE IA OE. **WOMAN HOLDING
A FRUIT.** 1893
Oil on canvas. 92 x 73 cm

formation of his creative system that brilliantly revealed itself in still-life, landscape and
portrait paintings. He rendered volumes and
forms not by means of light and shadow as
the Old Masters did, but by alternating warm
and cold shades of colour. Pursuing his difficult aims, he consciously made up his still-
life compositions of objects that were simple
in shape and allowed the painter to look for
their underlying geometrical forms — the
cone, the sphere and the cylinder. While depicting people, Cézanne never set the task to
convey their psychological state or character. Man was for him primarily the most complex and interesting form created by nature.
Cézanne partly drew his method of work on
landscapes from the Impressionists — he also
used the system of correlating warm and cold
colour shades underlying the Impressionist
method of painting. But the Impressionist
painters and Cézanne had a different perception of nature. Mount Sainte-Victoire near Aix,
to which Cézanne regularly went every day to
make his sketches, was, in his opinion, a majestic and harmonious work of nature, a perfect creation with its rhythms dominating the
surrounding space.

Impressionism gave an impetus for such a colourful and dramatic art as that of Vincent
van Gogh, A Dutchman by birth, Van Gogh
spent the most important and fruitful part of
his short and tragic life in France. The Hermitage owns four works by Van Gogh which
were painted during the last phase of his life,
at Arles and at Auvers-sur-Oise where he committed suicide. His *Lilac Bush* was painted in
May 1889 in the garden of the asylum at St Rémy,
near Arles, where the artist took cure after
one of his usual attacks of mental disease.
During a period of temporary relief Van Gogh
created this work, a true masterpiece of painting, imparting a heightened dramatic sense
and profound symbolic meaning to a common
study from nature. The painting *Cottages* was
produced at Auvers, where Dr. Paul Gachet
cured him in his clinic. The light colour scheme

based on the various relationships of warm ochreous and cold green-blue tints is full of harmony. Only the sharp and nervous impasto brushstrokes soaring upwards from the lower right-hand corner of the painting and joining a similar stream of strokes in the upper part of the canvas betray enormous spiritual tension. This picture makes us response to it, to echo the vibration of the artist's soul and to feel it in each dab, each line and each spot of the picture.

Gauguin was another seminal figure who foreshadowed, together with Cézanne and Van Gogh, twentieth-century art. He began his artistic career at the age of thirty-five. Being a prosperous broker, he took up painting as an amateur. The Impressionists were for the beginning artist his teachers, idols and friends. Gauguin even took part in the last three exhibitions of this artistic union. However, he soon evolved the individual manner of his own that was named by his contemporaries in different ways — Synthetism, Cloisonnism or Symbolism. Already early independent works by Gauguin are full of symbols and his new

159 / 160 / 161

HENRI MATISSE. 1869–1954
THE ARTIST'S FAMILY. 1911
Oil on canvas. 143 x 194 cm

HENRI MATISSE. 1869–1954
CONVERSATION. 1909
Oil on canvas. 177 x 217 cm

HENRI MATISSE. 1869–1954
**THE RED ROOM
(DESSERT. HARMONY IN RED).** 1908
Oil on canvas. 180 x 220 cm

painterly method based on daring combinations of bright colour spots encircled with firm lines was reminiscent of medieval technique of cloisonné enamel (hence one of the names of his techniques). Gauguin created his best works at Tahiti— an island of his dream, which he had sought for throughout his previous life and where he found a veritable earthly paradise inhabited by beautiful, natural and free people. He died in solitude on the small Dominique Island in the Pacific leaving after himself dozens of masterpieces that were not known to anybody and are now the pride of the world's leading museums. The Hermitage boasts a large collection of Gauguin's paintings — fifteen works created mainly at Tahiti Island. In his best works from this period the artist attained at last that harmony of which he had dreamed earlier, in Paris. He saw an image of a "Golden Age" in the quiet and natural tenure of life of the Maori people living at one with nature. The landscape in his *Pastorales Tahitiennes* is a powerful chord of resonant colour spots and the whimsical, meandering rhythm of its linear design seems to echo the sounds of a pipe played by the woman seated behind the tree. The colour and line are almost a palpable embodiment of music permeating this real Tahitian scene depicted as a dreamland. The painting *Woman Holding a Fruit* expresses Gauguin's ideal of beauty. The woman's face is quiet and immobile. She is reminiscent of a statue carved in wood and at the same time she

appears as a majestic and happy human being living amidst generous and primordial nature. The subjects of Gauguin's Tahitian canvases are complex and polysemantic, but all of them bear a stamp of the master's especial talent to infuse the inimitable feeling of life into the most rational and conventional idea.

The large collection of works by Matisse, a pride of the Hermitage, was, before the revolution of 1917, part of the unique private collection of Sergei Shchukin in Moscow. This collection enables us to follow the entire evolution of Matisse's work stage by stage. The earliest Matisses in the Hermitage collection date from the end of the nineteenth century. His *Blue Pot and Lemon* and *Fruit and Coffee-Pot* illustrate the artist's interest in Impressionism during his early years. At the turn of the century Matisse revealed an active interest in Gauguin's artistic quests as is confirmed by his another piece in the Hermitage collection, the landscape *The Luxembourg Gardens*. The works of 1905–07 (*View of Collioure, Lady on the Terrace*) show that they were created in the period when the artistic system of Fauvism had already been evolved. Matisse did not seek to record exactly the real colour — he liked to say that the Fauves took much from Impressionism, but the Impressionists drew their chromatic range from nature whereas he invented it himself." Matisse's colouristic programme was most fully realized in his monumental paintings without which it is impossible to form an idea of the scope of his creative accomplishments. These are primarily such

Hermitage masterpieces as *The Red Room*, *Conversation*, *The Artist's Family*, *The Dance* and *Music*. Each of them may be compared to an orchestra in which the solo part is given to some definite colour. In *The Red Room*, Matisse subordinated the three-dimensional volumes of objects to the plane of the canvas and transformed the figures of the woman, the vase of fruit, the carafes with vine, the trees and flowers into rhythmically bent colour spots making up a powerful colouristic chord with the blue pattern of the fascinating red fabric. The blue colour might be called the principal character in the painting *Conversation* — it dominates the entire space of the picture. However, the two figures, the seated woman and the standing man, are not merely plastic accents of the composition — the relationships between them are more complicated and emotionally profound. In the 1910s Matisse began to show a strong interest in the art of the Moslem East and the results of this infatuation left a specific trace in his art. Creating his monumental canvas *The Artist's Family*, Matisse was inspired by Persian miniatures. In the spring of 1909 the artist received a commission for two decorative panels from Sergei Shchukin. The panels were to adorn the staircase in the new mansion of the art patron in Moscow. Thus Matisse's famous ensemble of the two large-scale paintings, *The Dance* and *Music*, was created. It is but natural that the artist did not limit himself by purely decorative tasks in his work on these pictures. The seeming simplicity of its artistic solution conceals profound ideas and associations. The "dance" in Matisse's treatment is a symbolic action related to life and motion. The colours chosen for the painting symbolize the unity of the sky, earth and man.

162 / 163 / 164

HENRI MATISSE. 1869–1954
THE DANCE. Decorative panel. 1910
Oil on canvas. 260 x 391 cm

HENRI MATISSE. 1869–1954
VASE OF IRISES. 1912
Oil on canvas. 118 x 100 cm

HENRI MATISSE. 1869–1954
MUSIC. Decorative panel. 1910
Oil on canvas. 260 x 389 cm

The dashing rhythm of the naked bodies performing a round dance implies a link between the sky and earth and alludes to a magic primordial act, natural, free and dynamic. Here, like in *The Dance*, the action is set on a hill where, under the endless blue sky, beautiful sounds of music are spreading over the green land. Therefore these two companion works acquire their full sense and harmonic unity only when treated as a single whole.

Kees van Dongen, who had arrived in Paris from Holland, became a fashionable portrait painter introducing the public at large to a mysterious, extravagant and vicious world of the Parisian artistic Bohemians. His characters are *femmes fatales* obsessed by an idea to seduce, attract and amaze. Van Dongen makes use of saturated open colour combinations and close-ups. His works are marked by an air of garishness, a desire to strike at the first glance — the quality suggesting an affinity between his paintings and posters. However, the power of the artist's best works, including the Hermitage's *Lady in a Black Hat* and *Lucy and Her Partner*, lies in that behind the mask of a mysterious idol of the crowd one can feel the tragedy of solitude in the contemporary world. Landscapes painted by another Fauve, Maurice Vlaminck, Derain's close friend who shared a studio with him at Chatou in the suburbs of Paris, are full of dramatic tension. It is expressed in dynamic impasto brushstrokes and open combinations of deep blue, red and yellow colour shades. On passing a "test by colour" with the Fauves, Vlaminck revealed an inner kinship with Van Gogh and Cézanne in his best works. The work of Albert Marquet, in comparison with the mighty colourful symphonies of his friend Matisse, seems to be intimate and traditional. Like the Impressionists, Marquet sought to convey atmospheric effects but his painting is more concise, conventional and balanced. In his *Bay of Naples* Marquet reduces his palette to generalized spots of white, blue and black colour, but these modest means turn out to be sufficient

for rendering a sense of fresh sea air and a transparent atmosphere pervaded with light. Raoul Dufy also contributed to the Fauves' exhibitions and in the 1920s, similarly to Van Dongen, became a favourite artist of society salons. His work is distinguished by an ease and virtuoso elegance of execution, and a wonderful gift as a colourist. These qualities are equally visible in his numerous landscapes, portraits and large-scale decorative paintings. Dufy's *Regatta (Yachts in the Port of Dauville)*, now in the Hermitage collection, is also remarkable for its high artistic merits.

The Hermitage owns one of the world's most significant collections of works by Pablo Picasso, a great twentieth-century master. It includes over thirty paintings, works of sculpture, ceramics and graphic art. All the paintings produced by Picasso before the First World War represent three early, most fruitful phases in his work — the Blue, Pink and Cubist periods. The Hermitage's *Absinthe Drinker* was painted by Picasso at the age of twenty, sooon after his arrival in Paris from Spain. A tragic sense of hopelessness is vividly expressed in *The Visit (Two Sisters)*, a central work

165 / 166 / 167

KEES VAN DONGEN. 1877–1968
LADY IN A BLACK HAT. *Ca* 1908
Oil on canvas. 100 x 81 cm

RAOUL DUFY. 1877–1953
REGATTA (YACHTS IN THE PORT OF DAUVILLE). *Ca* 1936
Oil on canvas. 54 x 80.8 cm

MAURICE VLAMINCK. 1876–1958
VIEW OF THE SEINE. 1905–06
Oil on canvas. 54 x 64.5 cm

of the Blue period. In 1906 Picasso arrived at Cubism. He created within this trend his distinctive world based on the laws of geometry and logic. On the one hand, Cubism was based on the famous Cézanne's formula that everything in nature could be represented in the form of the sphere, the cylinder and the cone, but on the other, it drew from a geometrical simplicity and inner freedom of African sculpture. In Picasso's *Woman with a Fan (After the Ball)* all the details of the face and body are reduced to simplified forms and combinations of arc-shaped and rectangular volumes. However, the geometrical figure, seemingly cut out of hard rock, does not lose its emotional force — its pose and the gesture of the inclined head express a deep sense of tiredness and concentration. The superb Cubist images allow us to trace Picasso's creative evolution — from heavy geometricized figures of the Analytical period to the more elaborate arrangements of the so-called Synthetic phase of 1912–14. Picasso himself compared his later Cubist works with a cracked mirror. He seems to have broken objects in order to make up of their details new, previously unseen constructions. In his painting *Violin and Guitar* Picasso creates from fragments of musical instruments a new structure, both abstract and alive, subordinate to mysterious rhythms and laws determined by intuition. The canvas becomes the scene of an intellectual play of pure form, set free from the dictate of nature, which would become the foundation of the most radical twentieth-century movement — Abstract Art.

 168 / 169

PABLO PICASSO. 1881–1973
WOMAN WITH A FAN (AFTER THE BALL). 1908
Oil on canvas. 150 x 100 cm

PABLO PICASSO. 1881–1973
VIOLIN AND GUITAR. 1913
Oil on canvas. 65 x 54 cm

170

PABLO PICASSO. 1881–1973
ABSINTHE DRINKER. 1901
Oil on canvas. 73 x 54 cm

SPAIN

Before the early nineteenth century European collectors knew only several names of Spanish artists — Diego Velázquez, Hosé de Ribera and Bartolomé Estebán Murillo. The art of Murillo was especially popular in Russia in the eighteenth century. The artist's fame inspired Catherine the Great to purchase a number of his superb canvases for her Hermitage collection. A real interest in Spanish painting arouse only in the nineteenth century, after the Napoleonic Wars, when paintings by major artists, previously kept in the monasteries, cathedrals and palaces, began to be taken abroad from the devastated Spain and put on sale in Paris and London. It was then that the Hermitage accumulated its relatively not large, but fairly good, in comparison with the other museums of the world, Spanish collection comprising about 150 paintings. The main part of them are works representing the "Golden Age" of Spanish art — the seventeenth century. Spanish art developed in its own special way, different from that of neighbouring European countries. The year 1492 saw the successful end of the Reconquista, a liberation war led by the Spaniards against the Moors for more than eight centuries. Spain, which had gained independence, succeeded in capturing by the sixteenth century the New World and

several countries in North Africa, part of Italy and the Netherlands. In a century Spain became a very rich state. However, Spanish culture of the fifteenth century, with its marked dependence on medieval religious canons, was closed for the Renaissance ideas that had radically altered the culture of Italy and the Netherlands. Deep piety and loyalty to the ideals of Roman Catholic faith became the principal qualities of the Spanish national character and were naturally reflected in art. While strictly following canonic rules, Spanish religious painting was marked by an especial sincerity and expressiveness in the treatment of Christian subjects. Excellent examples of the art of this period are the Hermitage paintings made on panels. Originally they had been parts of *retablos* — large-scale church altars including paintings, pieces of sculpture and architectural details. It was not until the sixteenth century that the processes testifying to the gradual departure from the medieval canons began in Spanish painting. The only secular genre allowed in Spanish art during that period was formal portraiture. The Hermitage works by the leading Spanish portrait painter of the period Alonso Sánchez Coello and his pupil Juan Pantoja de la Cruz enable us to appreciate the refined aristocratic elegance and noble restraint characteristic of the best works of this kind.

The seventeenth century is usually regarded as the flourishing period of Spanish painting. Its beginning was marked by the great El Greco (Domenikos Theotoco-poulos), who came to Spain in the 1570s from Italy. Born on Crete, he arrived in Venice in his early years and began to work in the studio of Titian, studying also the art of Tintoretto and Veronese. In search of commissions he went to Rome where he received the news that King Philip II of Spain invited European masters for the decoration of the Escorial, his new residence. However, El Greco, as he was called in Spain because of his long name which was difficult to pronounce, did

THE NEW HERMITAGE
THE SPANISH SKYLIGHT ROOM

not become painter to the King. The freedom-loving master had to leave the official Madrid for Toledo that was in opposition to the royal court. The Hermitage owns two works by the famous artist. His portrait of the outstanding sixteenth-century poet Alonso de Ercilla y Zuñiga, was painted by El Greco probably before his arrival to Spain. El Greco's second, world-famous painting *The Apostles Peter and Paul*, is the earliest of his works created in Spain, at Toledo, and is part of the *apostolados* series dedicated to Christ and the Twelve Apostles. According to the Scriptures, the characters of Christ's disciples, Peter and Paul, were quite opposite. Peter was a simple and unsophisticated fisher, soft, meek and kind. Paul was of noble origin, educated, resolute and undaunted. The artist juxtaposes the two polar individualities emphasizing the difference of their characters by the contrasts of colour and rhythm.

The work of Hosé de Ribera opens up the era of the "Golden Age" in Spanish painting. Ribera spent most of his lifetime in Naples, which was then a part of the Spanish Kingdom. *St Jerome Listening to the Sounds of Trumpet* is one of Ribera's earliest signed works. The hermit is depicted at the moment when he heard the sound of the trumpet announcing the end of the world. In the semi-dark cell in which the saint was working only his face and figure and the angel, a messenger who brought the fearsome news, are highlighted. Ribera thoroughly conveys Jerome's old emaciated body and ascetically sunken eyes. The naturalistic details, however, do not prevent us from perceiving the image as a monumental and majestic one. Such heroic treatment of the images of Christian martyrs became a remarkable feature of Spanish religious painting in the seventeenth century.

The art of Diego Velázquez, the most celebrated Spanish artist, court painter to King Philip IV, is represented in the Hermitage by two paintings. *Luncheon*, an early work of the eighteen-year-old painter, belongs to the *bodegon* ("tavern") genre which was very popular in Spain. It was Caravaggio who introduced such scenes with so-called "cellar" illumination. The great Italian's works had

171 / 172 / 173

HOSÉ DE RIBERA. 1591–1652
ST JEROME LISTENING TO THE SOUNDS OF TRUMPET. 1626
Oil on canvas. 185 x 133 cm

JUAN PANTOJA DE LA CRUZ. 1553–1608
PORTRAIT OF DIEGO DE VILLAMAYOR. 1605
Oil on canvas. 89 x 71 cm

EL GRECO (DOMENIKOS THEOTOCOPOULOS). 1541–1614
THE APOSTLES PETER AND PAUL. Between 1587 and 1592
Oil on canvas. 121.5 x 105 cm

174 / 175 / 176

DIEGO VELÁZQUEZ. 1599–1660
LUNCHEON. *Ca* 1617–18
Oil on canvas. 108.5 x 102 cm

VASE. 16th century
Andalusia. Glass. Height 32 cm

DIEGO VELÁZQUEZ. 1599–1660
**PORTRAIT OF COUNT-DUKE
OF OLIVARES.** *Ca* 1640
Oil on canvas. 67 x 54.5 cm

a great impact on Spanish art. The early Velázquez also owed much to Caravaggio. Velázquez depicts a tavern scene with Spanish people having a modest meal and illuminated by a narrow stream of direct light, which singles the group out against the semi-dark interior. However, Velázquez invests this seemingly everyday scene, in the same way as Caravaggio before him, with some additional meaning. The still-life objects in the foreground — a pomegranate, a loaf and a glass of wine — are Christian symbols, and the images of the boy, youth and old man can be associated with the three periods in human life. The portrait of Count-Duke of Olivares ranks with undoubted masterpieces of Velázquez's portraiture. Don Gaspar de Guzmán, Count of Olivares, Duke of San Lucár, became the mighty Prime-Minister after the accession of the young Philip IV. It was thanks to Olivares that Velázquez received the position of court painter. The portrait, very simple and austere in composition, reflects the tragically contradictory character of the factual ruler of Spain.

The Spanish court, for which Velázquez worked as an artist, struck by its wealth and luxury. Portraits of Spanish aristocrats sometimes show amazingly beautiful and rare decorations — big emeralds, sapphires, pearls and golden objects brought from America. These pieces of jewellery later became rarities sought

after by art collectors. The Hermitage owns a unique pendant of Spanish work in the shape of caravel, produced at the end of the sixteenth century. The body of this marvellous and precious caravel is made of a huge solid emerald that was evidently brought to Spain from Columbia.

The Hermitage has four paintings by Francisco de Zurbarán. Worthy of special attention among them is the monumental altarpiece *St Laurent* painted for the Monastery of St Joseph in Seville. Zurbarán, following the national tradition, does not idealize the saint's image, but endows it with distinctive Spanish features. However, Zurbarán succeeded in creating a devotional image marked by an air of monumentality and significance. *The Girlhood of the Madonna* is one of a few lyrical paintings in the oeuvre of this usually austere master restrained in his emotions. His Virgin Mary, a black-haired and dark-eyed Spanish girl illuminated by a powerful stream of light pouring from above, seems to stiffen in a deep and silent ecstasy of prayer.

The Hermitage owns a representative collection of works by Bartolomé Esteban Murillo, which reflects all the phases of his work. Specialists single out three periods in Murillo's oeuvre — the *estile frio* ("cold"), the *estile calido* ("warm") and the *estile vaporoso* ("airy"). *The Boy with a Dog* dates from the early period when the artist worked in the *estile frio* and eagerly painted common people, tramps, gypsies and beggars clad in picturesque rags, who were poor yet optimistic and ingenious in revealing their feelings. *The Immaculate Conception*, a virtuoso painting in a light silver-blue gamut, is a perfect example of the artist's "airy" manner. Superb examples of Murillo's monumental religious painting are two canvases from the series dedicated to the Old Testament Prophet Jacob. The subject of *The Blessing of Jacob* was borrowed from the biblical story about the two brothers, Esau and Jacob, the sons of Isaac and Rebecca. The dramatic sense of the events treated in the picture seems to be of minor importance to the artist who focuses his attention on the landscape spread over almost a half of the immense composition. The space rendered in a virtuoso manner, with the subtlest colour and light nuances, makes this canvas one of the most superb examples of landscape painting dating from the seventeenth century.

An interest in the observation of real life was inherent to all the masters of the "Golden Age" of Spanish art. Genre scenes by the Madrid artist Antonio Puga usually capture not only individual

177 / 178 / 179

FRANCISCO DE ZURBARÁN. 1598–1664
THE GIRLHOOD OF THE VIRGIN. *Ca* 1660
Oil on canvas. 73.5 x 53.5 cm

BARTOLOMÉ ESTEBAN MURILLO. 1617–1682
THE IMMACULATE CONCEPTION. 1660s
Oil on canvas. 236 x 197 cm

FRANCISCO DE ZURBARÁN. 1598–1664
ST LAURENT. 1636
Oil on canvas. 292 x 225 cm

features of the characters portrayed, but the shades of their moods. The people in his canvas *Grinder* do not sit for him — they are concentrated on their activities and that is why their postures are so natural and easy. The artist depicts not grandees or noble hidalgos, but common people, emphasizing such

180 / 181 / 182

BARTOLOMÉ ESTEBAN MURILLO. 1617–1682
ISAAC BLESSING JACOB. 1665–1670s
Oil on canvas. 245 x 357.5 cm

ANTONIO PUGA. *Ca* 1602–1648
GRINDER
Oil on canvas. 118 x 158.5 cm

BARTOLOMÉ ESTEBAN MURILLO. 1617–1682
BOY WITH A DOG. 1650s
Oil on canvas. 74 x 60 cm

Spanish national features as the sense of inner dignity and restraint. The seventeenth century witnessed the flourishing of Spanish still life. Antonio da Pereda, one of the best Madrid painters of the mid-seventeenth century, seems to caress each object in his still life juxtaposing their textures and thus suggesting an invisible presence of man in the realm of *nature morte*.

The Hermitage's *Portrait of the Actress Antonia Zárate* is a work of the great Spanish artist Francisco de Goya, who completed the country's flourishing period in painting at the turn of the eighteenth and nineteenth centuries. The model's face, standing out against the dark background, is softly modelled by light and shade. Goya liked to finish his portraits under artificial lighting. So the colour scheme of the of the picture is based on the combination of contrasting red, blue and pearl-greyish tints rendering the textures of the transparent fabric and soft fur, the shades of the white skin and the glistening of the large black eyes. This emotional, touching image of a young woman links the spiritual world of Spanish art with the forthcoming age of Romanticism.

183 / 184

ANTONIO DE PEREDA. 1608–1678
STILL LIFE
Oil on canvas. 80 x 94 cm

FRANCISCO DE GOYA. 1746–1828
PORTRAIT OF THE ACTRESS ANTONIA ZÁRATE. *Ca* 1811
Oil on canvas. 71 x 58 cm

FLANDERS

The art of Flanders is exhaustively represented in the Hermitage. The museum possesses over 500 works in a variety of genres demonstrating the versatile mastery of Flemish artists — multifigure compositions of mythological, allegorical and religious content, portraits, still lifes, landscapes and genre scenes. The collection makes it possible to illustrate all the specific features of one of the leading seventeenth-century schools of art that contains more than 140 names. The Hermitage boasts large groups of paintings by the most significant Flemish masters whose works entered the museum as early as the reign of Catherine the Great. It has about forty works by the leader of the Flemish school Peter Paul Rubens, twenty-four works by the famous portrait painter Anthonis van Dyck, large-scale works by Frans Snyders, Jacob Jordaens and Paul de Vos, and genre scenes by David Teniers the Younger and Adriaen Brouwer. In the early nineteenth century the Hermitage's collection of Flemish painting had already rivalled the best similar collections throughout the world.

Flanders as an independent state emerged on the map of Europe in the early seventeenth century. After a prolonged war for liberation against Spain, which had ruled the Low Countries from the middle of the sixteenth century, seven northern provinces gained independence and proclaimed the Dutch Republic. In the Southern Netherlands, then known as Flanders, after the name of the largest province, the rule of the Spanish governor-general survived. From this time onwards these two parts of the previously single country went along different paths in their historical and cultural development. Netherlandish art fell apart into two independent national schools — Dutch and Flemish ones. The flowering of Flemish painting in the first half of the seventeenth century is associated primarily with Peter Paul Rubens. The head of the national school, he resolutely transformed the art of his country and guided it along a new course. Although Rubens himself worked mainly as a painter, the sphere of his influence involved all kinds of the fine arts — engraving, sculpture, architecture, decorative and applied art. His Antwerp studio

turned, to use the expression of his contemporaries, into "a kind of academy where one could reach the summits of art". Rubens created his own style that determined the specific features of Flemish painting, a style along the lines of which developed, while retaining their individual features, his numerous pupils and followers. The Hermitage collection enables us to fully estimate the entire scope of the great Flemish painter. Although Rubens himself asserted that he is more inclined to create huge canvases, his works in the Hermitage are represented in all variety of its forms and genres — altarpieces, sketches for large-scale decorative panels, portraits, landscapes and studies. Rubens began his creative career in Antwerp, but his travel to Italy exerted a great influence on the formation of the young artist. Even his early works replete with impressions from the art of Classical Antiquity and the Renaissance reveal the artist's deep originality: his characters embody the purely Flemish ideal of full-blooded beauty and vitality. Rubens took an active part in the creation of the Baroque style, which enabled him to express harmoniously his pantheistic world

THE NEW HERMITAGE
THE SNYDERS ROOM

185 / 186

PETER PAUL RUBENS. 1577–1640
PERSEUS AND ANDROMEDA. Early 1620s
Oil on canvas, transferred from a panel
99.5 x 139 cm

PETER PAUL RUBENS. 1577–1640
**PORTRAIT OF THE LADY-IN-WAITING
TO THE INFANTA ISABELLA.** Mid-1620s
Oil on canvas. 64 x 48 cm

perception and powerful temperament. The first commissioned works painted by the artist in Antwerp after his return from Italy struck his contemporaries by extraordinary expression, dynamism and the intensity of passion. During this period Rubens painted *The Roman Charity*, the subject which was connected with his Italian experience. The austere concise composition of *The Roman Charity* was certainly inspired by ancient reliefs. This heroic work illustrates a story about the selfless love of a young woman who fed her weakened father in a dungeon at her breast and thus saved him from hungry death. The Hermitage collection allows one to see a different, more profound and psychological facet of Rubens's talent. *Portrait of the Lady-in-Waiting* (mid-1620s) is one of the artist's unique pictures marked by a restraint, intimacy and compositional austerity unusual for his temperament. The girl's fragile image, marked by dreaminess and sorrow, has a touch of soft elegance and serenity about it; her face woven of the subtlest nuances of colour seems to be shining from within. Rubens painted *Perseus and Andromeda,* another masterpiece of the Hermitage collection, about 1622, when his art attained an unrivalled excellence. This painting, which has not lost the harmony and freshness of its colours almost four hundred years after its creation, is based on a mythological subject borrowed from Ovid's *Metamorphoses*. Such works, captivating by their turbulent energy and bright, rich colours, are characteristic of the artist's mature period to which most of the

Hermitage's works belong. Rubens's superb mastery permeates with living energy even the most conventional allegoric compositions. *The Union of Earth and Water* is a monumental allegory glorifying the union of two elements. The goddess Cybele personifies the Earth and the sea god Neptune symbolizes the Water. *Bacchus*, another masterpiece of the Hermitage collection, ranks with the best works of Rubens's later period. Here Rubens turns again to a mythological subject freely interpreting it in accordance with his own notions of the "Golden Age" of the ancient civilization. The artist shows the ancient god of wine not in his usual image of a beautiful young man but as a fat reveller seated on a barrel amidst his drunken suite of satyrs and bacchantes. Bacchus seems to concentrate in himself the powerful, unbridled, elemental powers of nature; he is the apotheosis of human flesh, a celebration of the inexhaustible fertility of the earth. Rubens's mastery as a painter attains in *Bacchus* its consummation. The master models the form in sweeping brushstrokes emphasizing the golden-coloured mass of the god's stout body and the light tender flesh of the bacchantes and *putti,* and fills the space of the painting with a soft light linking the figures with the landscape. The colour gamut here has completely lost its local character and the numerous

187 / 188 / 189

PETER PAUL RUBENS. 1577–1640
THE UNION OF EARTH AND WATER. *Ca* 1618
Oil on canvas. 222.5 x 180.5 cm

PETER PAUL RUBENS. 1577–1640
**THE ROMAN CHARITY
(CIMON AND PERO).** *Ca* 1612
Oil on canvas, transferred from a panel
140.5 x 180.3 cm

PETER PAUL RUBENS. 1577–1640
BACCHUS. Between 1638 and 1640
Oil on canvas, transferred from a panel
191 x 161.3 cm

shades put close to one another merge into a unified sonorous and elaborate chord. Of exceptional value is the Hermitage collection of Rubens's sketches not infrequently surpassing in their mastery and freedom of execution finished works.

The twenty-four Hermitage's paintings by Anthonis van Dyck), who won fame as the best portraitist of Europe during his young years, demonstrate diverse facets of his talent. Of great importance for the young master was his work with Rubens. Overloaded with commissions, Rubens usually entrusted the most important parts of his large-scale paintings to Van Dyck — as a rule the principal assistant painted the heads of numerous characters in works commissioned from the master. Van Dyck's own works, nevertheless, betray a distinctive individuality. The Hermitage portraits by Van Dyck belong to different periods of his creative career and are markedly different in the manner of execution. He painted *Family Portrait* about 1621, before his departure for Italy. In its outward features it is still closely linked with the traditional Netherlandish type of representation. The six-year sojourn in Italy, which began in 1621, polished the artist's talent to perfection. Under the influence of great Italian masters of the Renaissance, especially Titian, Tintoretto and Veronese, his favourite Venetians, Van Dyck noticeably enriched his palette with bright, varicoloured and saturated tones. Having evolved a special type of formal aristocratic portrait-picture, the Flemish artist enjoyed world-wide renown. On his return to Antwerp Van Dyck created magnificent examples of portrait art among which the Hermitage's *Self-Portrait* is worthy of special note. The refinement and elegance, which distinguish Van Dyck's mature

190 / 191 / 192

ANTHONIS VAN DYCK. 1599–1641
FAMILY PORTRAIT. Late 1621
Oil on canvas. 113.5 x 93.5 cm

ANTHONIS VAN DYCK. 1599–1641
**PORTRAIT OF THE COURT LADIES ANNE DALKEITH,
COUNTESS OF MORTON (?), AND ANNE KERK.** Late 1630s
Oil on canvas. 131.5 x 150.6 cm

ANTHONIS VAN DYCK. 1599–1641
SELF-PORTRAIT. Late 1620s – early 1630s
Oil on canvas. 116.5 x 93.5 cm

period, can be keenly felt in this self-portrait. The artist apparently idealizes his own image, representing himself as a handsome and romantic young man nonchalantly resting his arm on the base of a column. In 1620, before Van Dyck's departure for Italy, King James I of England, charmed by his work, invited the artist to London. But the young Fleming, on becoming a "servant of His Majesty", spent in England only several months. In 1632, four years after his return from Italy, Van Dyck left his native Antwerp for London, where he became court painter to Charles I. This last, short period is especially well represented in the Hermitage collection. The artist usually employed several basic compositional devices in his formal portraits of the English period. In his *Portrait of Sir Thomas Wharton* Van Dyck placed the sitter wearing a bright suit sparkling with precious silks against a characteristic English landscape with a bright, cloudy sky. Van Dyck's double portrait of the court ladies Anne Dalkeith, Countess of Morton (?), and Anne Kerk is notable for its strikingly harmonious colour

193 / 194 / 195

JACOB JORDAENS. 1593–1678
THE BEAN KING. *Ca* 1638
Oil on canvas. 157 x 211 cm

FRANS SNYDERS. 1579–1657
FRUIT ON THE TABLE
Oil on panel. 71.6 x 103 cm

FRANS SNYDERS. 1579–1657
FISH SHOP
Oil on canvas. 207 x 341 cm

range and variety of tints. The artist effectively and at the same time elegantly combined subtle silvery-greys with red, golden and black tones. It is apparent that Van Dyck does not idealize the appearance of his sitters very much, but as members of the aristocracy they are full of dignity and proud majesty. Van Dyck died and was buried in England, but the great Flemish artist has forever remained linked with his native country. No less remarkable figure in the history of Flemish art was the seventeenth-century painter Jacob Jordaens. His most famous work in the Hermitage's collection is *The Bean King* featuring a popular folk festival the "Feast of the Bean King" celebrated in Flanders on 6 January. During this day a large pie was baked in every home, with a bean put inside. The one who would find the bean in his piece of pie, was honoured as the "king" of the holiday. A "queen" and a "suite" were chosen for him from among the guests and when he lifted his goblet, everybody was supposed to join the chorus shouting: "The king is drinking!" and immediately empty his goblet to escape a joking fine.

Frans Snyders was also one of Rubens's assistants for many years. He became particularly famous as the painter of the *Shops* series now in the Hermitage. It consists of the four huge canvases painted for the decoration of a dining-room in the house of Archbishop Anthony in Bruges. Not a single European school of the seventeenth century has created anything on a par with these large-scale vigorous still lifes which seem to amass all the wealth of nature's riches — Snyders was justly called the "Rubens of still life".

175

HOLLAND

The first paintings by Dutch artists appeared in St Petersburg long before the foundation of the Hermitage. In 1716 Peter the Great acquired in Holland about two hundred works which were used to adorn his residence in the capital and suburban palaces. The Russian Tsar, as an adherent of the Dutch mode of life and culture, especially highly appreciated, according to Jacob von Stählin, scenes from the life of "Dutch peasant men and women" and therefore superb works by genre painters such as Jan Steen, Adriaen van Ostade and Philips Wouwerman were brought to Russia during that period. Peter's collection also included one of Rembrandt's masterpieces, *David and Jonathan*, the first work by the great master to come to Russia. Paintings by Dutch artists were always very popular with collectors and by the early twentieth century the Hermitage had possessed one of the largest collections of Dutch art. Nowhere else beyond the borders of Holland is the Dutch school represented with such completeness as in the Hermitage. A special feature of the collection, besides its huge size (over a thousand paintings) and a number of recognized masterpieces, is that great masters are displayed here amidst less prominent artists whose works are sometimes rare even in Dutch collections. The seventeenth century is often called the "Golden Age" of Dutch culture. This period was marked by a powerful upsurge in the economical, political and spiritual life of the country. The Dutch school of painting was formed later than the Flemish one — by the 1630s, and the period of

its highest development fell on the middle of the seventeenth century. Most of the artists (they are often called the "Small Dutch Masters") worked on commissions from local burghers, who preferred to adorn the rooms of their homes, not large in size, with small paintings — scenes of everyday life, portraits exactly conveying the appearance of real Dutchmen, still lifes of objects surrounding them and accustomed landscapes. The "art of reality" — portraiture, landscape, still life and genre scenes — was widespread in Holland and had a distinct national flavour. Each artist specialized in some definite field. Paintings by the "Small Dutch Masters" attracted not by their subjects alone, but by their complex colour schemes, virtuoso rendering of light and air medium and textural variety of objects in which seventeenth-century Dutch painters were unrivalled.

Gerard Terborch, a superb colourist and a keen observer of the life of his contemporaries, is represented in the Hermitage by six excellent works. The best of these paintings is surely *A Glass of Lemonade*. The artist has turned a scene with a procuress introducing a girl to a young soldier into a subtle and elevated world dominated by exquisite combinations of black, grey, golden and lemon shades. Gabriel Metsu, influenced by both Steen and Terborch, combined in his work a democratic and vivid approach of the former with an elegance of the latter.

THE NEW HERMITAGE
THE REMBRANDT ROOM

The theme of the painting *The Sick Woman and Her Doctor* was one of the most popular subjects occurring in many works by Dutch genre painters. Metsu, however, treats it in a deliberately theatrical and comically majestic manner — the doctor with a dignified air demonstrates a vessel with urine to a sick girl lying in an armchair. Usually such illnesses depicted in the works of Dutch artists were diagnosed as love disease and the subjects themselves as illustrations to the proverb: "Medicine is helpless where love is involved."

Frans van Mieris the Elder developed his techniques of miniature painting to unseen perfection. His pictures are marked by an utmost smoothness and a meticulous care for detail. *A Morning of Young Lady* is his veritable masterpiece. All details in the painting, bathed in sunlight, look almost tangible and three-dimensional. As is often the case with the Dutch genre artists, usual objects have an allegorical sense — a love letter on the table, fashionable shoes on the stairs and the lady's playing with a dog itself allude to a love adventure.

The great portrait painter of the seventeenth century Frans Hals is represented in the Hermitage by two outstanding examples of his work. Hals not only records the appearance of his model in sweeping, virtuoso brushstrokes, without indulging in elaboration of detail, but also captures the instantly changing features of the character portrayed. The artist demonstrates in his portraits the pose, gesture, turn of the head and look characteristic of this person alone in a definite situation. At the same time all the characters depicted by Hals have something in common — they share energetic, frank attitude to life. This is how A *Young Man with a Glove* looks like: a vivid glitter in his eyes, a smile that is going to appear on his lips, his hands captured in movement. The dynamism of the image is emphasized by brushstrokes, now small and merging into a whole as on the face, and now sweeping and divided as on the gloves, the collar lace and the curls of the young man.

The outstanding accomplishments of Dutch still-life painters are exemplified in the Hermitage by the works of major masters of this kind of painting — Pieter Claesz, Willem Claesz Heda and Willem Kalf. Their mastery is fully revealed in the so-called "breakfast" scenes. The type

196 / 197 / 198

GERARD TERBORCH. 1617–1681
A GLASS OF LEMONADE
Oil on canvas, transferred from a panel. 67 x 54 cm

FRANS JANSZ VAN MIERIS THE ELDER. 1635–1681
MORNING OF A YOUNG LADY. *Ca* 1659–60
Oil on panel. 51.5 x 39.5 cm

GABRIEL METSU. 1629–1667
THE SICK WOMAN AND HER DOCTOR. 1660s
Oil on canvas. 61.5 x 47.5 cm

of "breakfast" still life developed from early Netherlandish group portraits of corporate members in which the forefront usually showed laid tables with an abundance of diverse hors-d'oeuvres. In Holland this genre became more modest and intimate. An overturned goblet, a creased tablecloth, scattered knives, forks and spoons suggest in Dutch still-life paintings a presence of man who seems to have just left the room a minute before. The subtly harmonized colour range is characteristic of *Breakfast with Ham* by Pieter Claesz. The variegated local colours typical of early Dutch still lifes are ousted by restrained silvery tints pervaded with soft light and shade effects which reveal the texture of the objects. Willem Claesz Heda is another leading master of this genre. Objects in his still lifes are almost devoid of bright colours. The zinc jars, tin plates, transparent glassware, and silver or gilt goblets create a colour chord of impeccable harmony and beauty enhanced by the grey background saturated with light and the white tablecloth.

The work of Willem Kalf testifies to the change of taste that took place in Dutch society in the second half of the seventeenth century. The burghers who became rich were now trying to decorate their homes with objects of applied art and paintings attesting to their wealth. *Dessert*, Kalf's true masterpiece, is usually put into the category of "luxurious

199 / 200 / 201

FRANS HALS. Between 1581 and 1585 – 1666
**PORTRAIT OF A YOUNG MAN
WITH A GLOVE.** *Ca* 1650
Oil on canvas. 80 x 66.5 cm

WILLEM CLAESZ HEDA.
1594 – between 1680 and 1682
BREAKFAST. 1652
Oil on panel. 63 x 76 cm

WILLEM KALF. 1619–1693
DESSERT
Oil on canvas. 105 x 87.5 cm

still lifes". The traditional Dutch "breakfast" scene is filled here with valuable exotic objects: the artist arranges on the tablecloth a high gilt Augsburg cup, a vessel of green glass and an elegant thin goblet — the three vertical accents articulating the composition. The soft diffused light seems to penetrate into the depth of the objects revealing a striking variety and wealth of the textures: laid on the Chinese platter are succulent oranges, peaches and plums. The lemon peel hanging down from the plate to the shimmering silver dish unites all the details of this beautiful realm.

Landscape paintings by the "Small Dutch Masters" usually feature unassuming corners of the Dutch countryside. The flat even space conquered by people from the sea is not distinguished by any special colouristic effects, but the Dutch painters were particularly successful

202 / 203 / 204 / 205

JOST CORNELISZ DROOCHSLOOT. 1586–1666
WINTER IN A DUTCH TOWN
Oil on panel. 50.5 x 74.5 cm

JAN PORCELLIS. *Ca* 1584–1632
SEA ON A DULL DAY
Oil on panel. 47.5 x 63.5 cm

JACOB ISAACSZ VAN RUISDAEL. 1628/29–1682
MARSH. 1660s
Oil on canvas. 72.5 x 99 cm

JAN VAN GOYEN. 1596–1656
**WINTER LANDSCAPE IN THE ENVIRONS
OF THE HAGUE.** 1645
Oil on panel. 52 x 70 cm

in their efforts to convey the beauty and grandeur of their native countryside. The best qualities of Dutch landscape painting from the first half of the seventeenth century are embodied in the art of Jan van Goyen, who is represented in the Hermitage by twelve works. Each object in his painting seems to be tangible — the thoroughly worked out pearly-grey tonal colour range creates a sense of a unified light and air medium. The artist attains a true compositional perfection in his *Winter Landscape in the Environs of The Hague*: the ultimately low horizon allows him to convey the flat space receding into the distance and filled with the "living" figures of men and animals. The earth and the sky blend together into a coherent dynamic whole where the sky bears a greater emotional charge. The sea with which the life of any Dutchman was usually connected brought into being a special kind of landscape known as marine. Jan Porcellis was a Fleming by birth, but seascapes acquired distinctly Dutch features in his creative work. The sea and the sky, saturated with moisture, light, reflexes and shades, the light-and-air perspective — all this created a unified tonal medium that was especially favourable for revealing the harmony of silvery hues discovered in the scenery by Dutch painters. The highest accomplishments of Dutch landscape painting are associated with Jacob van Ruisdael, an outstanding artist whose works show a profound philosophic interpretation of nature. Ruisdael's landscapes evoke a feeling of majestic beauty and enormous living force, they seem to have been intended to encourage man's noble feelings and thoughts. The Hermitage owns eleven landscape paintings by Ruisdael. The best-known of them is *Marsh*, a true masterpiece of world painting. The monumental landscape, full of energy and grandeur, seems to be a hymn to the beauty of nature. Ruisdael, however, introduced a motif of inevitable decay into this majestic picture: the rotting stump of a once mighty birch in the foreground,

206

JAN STEEN. 1625/26–1679
REVELLERS. *Ca* 1660
Oil on panel. 39 x 30 cm

207 / 208

ISAACK JANSCZ VAN OSTADE. 1621–1649
READING A LETTER. *Ca* 1640
Oil on panel. 37.5 x 48.5 cm

ADRIAN VAN OSTADE. 1610–1685
BRAWL. 1637
Oil on panel. 25 x 33.5 cm

the bare branches of an oak-tree broken by the elements, the stiff surface of the bog into which fallen leaves are sinking. This real and at the same time generalized image of nature typifies the very essence of everything alive — birth, flowering, maturity and death.

The Hermitage possesses twenty-five paintings by Adriaen van Ostade, the greatest representative of the so-called peasant genre, who was active at Haarlem. *Brawl* is one of Ostade's most famous works. The peasants in his picture look like ugly, miserable creatures feverishly striking heavy blows with their fists. The caricature-like depiction of the characters with a stress on their brutality contrasts with a subtle colour range based on the rich shades of cold bluish and warm ochreous tints. Ostade makes the traditional genre more democratic bringing it down to

209 / 210

PIETER JANSSENS ELINGA. 1623–1682
ROOM IN A DUTCH HOUSE
Oil on canvas. 61.5 x 59 cm

PIETER DE HOOCH. 1629 – after 1684
MISTRESS AND HER MAID. *Ca* 1660
Oil on canvas. 53 x 42 cm

the level of a merry joke or amusing anecdote. His everyday scenes of peasant life — *Village Festival, Conversation by a Fire, Village Musician* — are permeated with a good-natured humour and a keen sense of reality.

Paintings by Jan Steen, the wittiest and most observant Dutch artist, are scenes from the life of common Dutchmen usually invested with some moral ideas, not indulging, though, either in crudeness or in moralizing. The painting *Revellers* is one of Steen's masterpieces. The amusing and lively characters in this painting are the artist himself and his wife Margaret, daughter of the landscape painter Jan van Goyen. Each detail of the composition is emphatically material, but the talented painter skilfully unites numerous objects into a single coherent structure. The subject looks like a well-performed mise-en-scène where both characters are exceedingly natural and harmonious. As is usual with Steen, this amusing situation conceals a moral maxim about pernicious consequences of the improper mode of life.

Pieter de Hooch succeeded in penetrating to the very essence of the Dutch burgher's personality lovingly emphasizing such features as harmony, calm and purity. The main character of his paintings is light pervading accurate Dutch interiors, courtyards and streets and revealing the beauty of the most common details — dresses, tableware, brickwork, foliage or the smooth water of a canal. The work of Pieter de Hooch exerted a great influence on many Dutch artists who worked in Delft and

211 / 212 / 213

REMBRANDT HARMENSZ VAN RIJN. 1606–1669
DANAË. 1636
Oil on canvas. 185 x 202.5 cm

REMBRANDT HARMENSZ VAN RIJN. 1606–1669
YOUNG WOMAN TRYING EARRINGS. 1657
Oil on panel. 39.5 x 32.5 cm

REMBRANDT HARMENSZ VAN RIJN. 1606–1669
FLORA. 1634
Oil on canvas. 125 x 101 cm

Amsterdam and primarily on Pieter Janssens Elinga, active between 1650 and 1670. The Hermitage's *Room in a Dutch House*, bathed in a bright sunlight that lends a festive, life-asserting appearance to a typically Dutch interior, ranks with the artist's best works.

The Hermitage collection of works by Rembrandt, the greatest Dutch master, an artist of genius, can be called unique without any reservation. More than twenty paintings (some of them were probably executed with an assistance of Rembrandt's pupils) cover various phases in the master's complicated career throughout forty year. The collection begins with his early works, still painted in a traditional meticulous manner and winning success with the public, and ends with the philosophically profound and tragic later images which were understood only by rare like-minded people. Created in different years, Rembrandt's paintings *The Sacrifice of Abraham*, *Flora*, *David and Jonathan*, *Danaë*, *The Holy Family* and *David and Uriah (?)* are his most important works eloquently expressing his creative credo. At the same time these masterpieces demonstrate those peculiar features of his pictorial idiom which markedly differentiated Rembrandt from his Dutch contemporaries during his mature period. Turning to remote Old and New Testament scenes and ancient myths, Rembrandt invested them with a profound dramatic feeling converting his characters into real, loving and suffering people. Almost half of Rembrandt's works in the Hermitage are portraits among which his likenesses of old men painted during his later years are especially remarkable for their psychological penetration. Most of them were painted not as commissions, but for himself — it was an expressive appearance and character of the models that primarily attracted the artist. Rembrandt's *Portrait of an Old Man in Red* ranks with his most outstanding works. He shows an old man seated motionlessly in an armchair and engrossed in his thoughts. The deep brushstrokes model his austere wrinkled face, his tired gnarled hands. It seems that a stream of reminiscences passes before the mental view of the old man who had learned much in life. A deep sense of maternal love,

214 / 215 / 216

REMBRANDT HARMENSZ VAN RIJN. 1606–1669
ABRAHAM'S SACRIFICE. 1635
Oil on canvas. 193 x 132 cm

REMBRANDT HARMENSZ VAN RIJN. 1606–1669
THE HOLY FAMILY. 1645
Oil on canvas. 117 x 91 cm

REMBRANDT HARMENSZ VAN RIJN. 1606–1669
PORTRAIT OF AN OLD MAN IN RED. *Ca* 1652–54
Oil on canvas. 108 x 86 cm

family warmth, calm and harmony permeates Rembrandt's painting *The Holy Family*. He depicted as the Madonna a common Dutch woman, Hendrikje Stoeffels, who substituted mother to Rembrandt's son Titus after the death of the artist's wife, Saskia. The warm, saturated colour range, rich in shades and composed of cinnabar-red, brown and golden-ochreous tones, the pigment laid onto canvas in pastoso strokes, the light pouring onto the figure of the mother and child seem to materialize the most beautiful human emotions. Rembrandt's later biblical subjects are distinguished by their utmost terseness of expression: they have no inner action and almost lack any details of setting. *David and Uriah (?)* is full of tragic inner tension. Its pictorial mastery stresses the artist's psychological penetration in the treatment of the theme unusual for that period. Uriah, doomed to die according to the will of King David who has fallen in love with his wife Bathsheba, is shown at a close-up, approaching the spectator. The king depicted behind his back seems to begin to repent his evil deed; the face of an old scribe exudes a deep suffering. The large painting *The Return of the Prodigal Son* is a great summation of Rembrandt's thoughts on the sense of life and the utmost evocation of his pictorial mastery. The subject of the Gospel parable about a prodigal son attracted many European artists. Rembrandt was the only of them who understood, during the last years of his life, the profound sense of this parable told by Christ. The artist chose the final episode of the story — the repentant sinner's return to the home of his parents and his meeting with his father. Rembrandt highlights in the deep dark space only the most important details — the old man's blind face devoid of any outer emotions, his vibrant hands put onto the back of his beloved, long-awaited son and the immobile figure of the reckless son, kneeling in deep repentance before his father. The colour scheme of the painting is limited to the combinations of red, ochreous and brown shades with a great wealth of the subtlest nuances within this sparing palette. When applying pigments on to the canvas, Rembrandt used a brush, a palette-knife, the handle of the brush and even his fingers, which heightened the vibrancy of the painted surface. The colours now grow more dense, radiating tension and energy and now seem to be lighted from within conveying the emotional state of the characters. This outstanding painting became an embodiment of Rembrandt's thoughts about man's principal spiritual values — a capacity to love and forgive. The huge canvas, which has nothing extraneous about it and in which the colour, light and even the painted texture itself seem to have acquired a spiritual quality, is the culmination of the great Dutch master's artistic career.

217 / 218 / 219

REMBRANDT HARMENSZ VAN RIJN. 1606–1669
DAVID AND URIAH (?). *Ca* 1665
Oil on canvas. 127 x 116 cm

REMBRANDT HARMENSZ VAN RIJN. 1606–1669
DAVID AND JONATHAN. 1642
Oil on panel. 73 x 61.5 cm

REMBRANDT HARMENSZ VAN RIJN. 1606–1669
THE RETURN OF THE PRODIGAL SON. *Ca* 1668–69
Oil on canvas. 262 x 205 cm

ENGLAND

Russia was probably the only country in Europe that revealed a serious interest in English art in the eighteenth century. Eminent English architects and gardeners took part in the creation of magnificent complexes of palaces and parks in the Russian capital and in its environs. Items of English art, which was in vogue during that period, were eagerly bought to enrich the collection of Catherine the Great and the St Petersburg aristocratic homes. English painting was then little known beyond the borders of the country. However, the famous collection of Sir Robert Walpole bought by Catherine the Great included a number of works by the owner's compatriots, which made up the kernel of the future Hermitage collection of English art. By the end of the century it was enlarged with several well-known works by famous English masters, notably Sir Joshua Reynolds and Joseph Wright of Derby. The nineteenth century witnessed a growth of an interest in English art, and works by painters from the British Isles could now be seen in numerous private collections. Several painters, attracted by the wealth and generosity of the Russian aristocracy, used to come to St Petersburg in search of profitable commissions. The creative career of the portraitist George Dawe,

who painted a large series of portraits of participants in the war against Napoleon, is connected with St Petersburg and the Winter Palace. In the 1830s to 1850s, the well-known Salon artist Christina Robertson, a typical representative of the official Victorian style, had a large high-ranking clientele at the Russian court. In 1912 the Picture Gallery of the Hermitage received a generous gift — a collection of English painting by the well-known St Petersburg art collector and Anglophile Alexei Khitrovo bequeathed to the gallery by its owner. The Hermitage received with this collection fine works by leading English portrait painters of the eighteenth and early nineteenth centuries, notably likenesses by Thomas Gainsborough, George Romney, John Hoppner, Henry Raeburn, John Opie and Thomas Lawrence. The majority of works that can be seen in the Hermitage display rooms devoted to English painting are portraits. This reflects the specific character of English art — starting from the period of the establishment of portraiture in the sixteenth century, it was considered the leading branch of art. England entered the period of the national Renaissance rather late, in the second half of the sixteenth century. However, national painting did not yield men of genius equal to the great playwright William Shakespeare or the philosophers Francis Bacon and Thomas More. For a long time painting did not occupy a predominant place in British culture. The original phase in the development of national painting was associated with the great German painter Hans Holbein the Younger who was invited to London by King Henry VIII in 1526. Holbein lived in London more than ten years and the masterpieces of portraiture he created became a real, if unattainable, school of craftsmanship for his English contemporaries and followers. Names of local

THE WINTER PALACE
THE ROOM OF ENGLISH ART: 16th and 17th Centuries

artists are rare in English painting of that period —
as a rule, painters came to England from the Netherlands or Germany. The portraits from the late
sixteenth and early seventeenth centuries represented in the Hermitage collection, which are
exceedingly rare beyond the boundaries of England, are ascribed to Hans Eworth and Marcus
Geeraerts the Younger, artists of Netherlandish
extraction. The next, no less significant event in
the artistic life of England was the arrival to London of the famous Flemish artist Anthonis van
Dyck, who was invited by King Charles I in the
1620s. The English consider Van Dyck to be the
founder of their national school of painting. Towards the end of the seventeenth century and
the beginning of the eighteenth English painting
came to the period of its flowering connected with
three outstanding artists — William Hogarth,
Joshua Reynolds and Thomas Gainsborough. Unfortunately, the Hermitage does not possess any
works by Hogarth.

Joshua Reynolds was the most influential English
painter of his time, the first President of the Academy of Arts. He is revered in his homeland as a
great portrait painter and an outstanding theo-
retician of art. Reynolds is represented in the
Hermitage collection by historical genre compositions, which are quite rare in his work. In December 1785 he received a flattering offer from the
Russian court to paint two large-scale paintings
on historical subjects. One of them was intended
for Catherine the Great and the other for Prince
Potemkin-Tavrichesky. For Catherine the Great,

220 / 221 / 222

JOSHUA REYNOLDS. 1723–1792
CUPID UNTYING THE GIRDLE OF VENUS. 1788
Oil on canvas. 127.5 x 101 cm

JOSHUA REYNOLDS. 1723–1792
**THE INFANT HERCULES STRANGLING
THE SERPENTS SENT BY HERA.** 1786–88
Oil on canvas. 303 x 297 cm

BENJAMIN WEST. 1738–1820
VENUS CONSOLING CUPID STUNG BY A BEE
Oil on canvas. 77 x 64 cm

Reynolds borrowed a subject from classical mythology and invested it with a remarkable meaning: this scene is an allegory glorifying the might of the young Russian state. The artist was inspired for the creation of this painting by the story of the Infant Hercules borrowed from an ode by the Greek poet Pindar. According to the myth, the jealous wife of Zeus, the ruler of the Olympian gods, decided to kill Hercules, son of Zeus and the mortal woman Alcmene, by sending into the crib of the sleeping infant two giant snakes. Hercules, who awoke from touches of cold snake bodies, strangled the serpents. In 1789 the work estimated as the best creation of the aging master by English critics, was dispatched to the capital of Russia. Catherine the Great was very pleased by this acquisition. The two other paintings, *The Continence of Scipio* and *Cupid Untying the Girdle of Venus*, which arrived in St Petersburg together with *The Infant Hercules Strangling the Serpents* for Prince Potemkin, also finally found their way to the Hermitage after his death in 1792. Reynolds's painting showing Venus and Cupid, the artist's replica of the famous work of 1784 now at the Tate Gallery in London, can be classed as a mythological subject only with a great degree of reservation. It is a fine example of a free improvisational manner and the artist's amazingly rich palette. The vibrant combinations of saturated reds, yellows and blues recall Reynolds's interest in colouristic developments of the great sixteenth-century Venetian painters, notably Titian. Venus painted by Reynolds is far from the ideal of classical beauty — her image is based on a representation of a smart red-haired English model, romantic and beautiful, affectedly shielding her face.

The same characters, Venus and Cupid, are depicted in the small-scale painting *Venus Consoling Cupid Stung by a Bee*,

223 / 224 / 225

GEORGE ROMNEY. 1734–1802
PORTRAIT OF MRS. HARRIET GREER. 1781
Oil on canvas. 76 x 64 cm

THOMAS GAINSBOROUGH. 1727–1788
PORTRAIT OF A LADY IN BLUE. Late 1770s
Oil on canvas. 76 x 64 cm

THOMAS LAWRENCE. 1769–1830
**PORTRAIT OF COUNT
MIKHAIL VORONTSOV.** 1821
Oil on canvas. 143 x 113 cm

the work of Benjamin West, an American by birth, who settled in England in 1763. The artist borrowed his subject from the ode *The Wounded Cupid* by the ancient Greek poet Anacreon. As a true adherent of Classicism, engrossed with a "reconstruction" on canvas of ideal ancient images, West carefully but coldly delineated a slender sculptural profile of the goddess of love. However, the image of a capricious and lovely Cupid and the light pink-bluish colour scheme lend to this love scene a somewhat sugary, sentimental flavour.

A marvel of the Hermitage's collection of painting is *Portrait of a Lady in Blue* by Gainsborough. Thomas Gainsborough ranks with the most brilliant painters of the eighteenth century. His painting is remarkable for a wealth of shades and a virtuoso craftsmanship, but at the same time his models are distinguished by a special refinement, poetic quality and elevated feelings — the features which were fully inherent to the artist himself. The *Portrait of a Lady in Blue* was painted in the 1770s, the period of flowering in Gainsborough's artistic career. The painter's mastery and a rare charm of the image he portrayed

226 / 227 / 228 / 229

INTAGLIO: *MARS AND BELLONA.* *Ca* 1784
By Charles Brown
Cornelian, in a golden mount. 4.1 x 3.5 cm

INTAGLIO: *THE HEAD OF HYGEIA.* *Ca* 1785
By William Brown
Cornelian, in a golden mount. 3 x 2.7 cm

WINE COOLER. 1734–35
London. By Charles Kandler
Cast in silver, chased. 100 x 169 x 98 cm

PIECES FROM THE GREEN FROG SERVICE. 1773–74
Josiah Wedgwood's Etruria Potteries, England
Creamware, painted in colours

never fail to attract the attention of visitors to the museum. "If ever the nation should produce genius sufficient to acquire to us the honourable distinction of an English School, the name of Gainsborough will be transmitted to posteriority in the history of Art, among the very first of that rising fame," wrote about this superb portrait painter Joshua Reynolds, his principal rival.

Joseph Wright of Derby is rightly reckoned one of the most original English painters of the eighteenth century. The circle of his themes included the subjects that were often thought to be far from the tasks of painting. Wright, who lived in Derby, a large industrial centre, was friendly with well-known scientists, inventors, philosophers and men of letters. He was interested in scenes of daily life that would allow him to convey the importance of man's physical life and its environment. One of such paintings is his work *An Iron Forge Viewed from Without*. The artist transformed the subject taken from real life into a poetic, even somewhat mysterious romantic elegy. The focus of Wright's interest was a whimsical play of light and shade in nature rather than people. The picture won a great popularity in England and was bought in the artist's studio specially for the collection of Catherine the Great.

Thomas Lawrence shared the glory of the outstanding eighteenth-century English portraitists. The recognition of his talent went far beyond the borders of his native country. Almost all crowned persons, diplomats and army leaders of Europe thought it honourable to seat for the celebrated English master of portraiture bestowed with the title of Painter to the Crown. The Hermitage's portraits of members of the well-known Russian family of Count Vorontsov allow us to appreciate the exceptional talent of the artist capable to see behind outward effects and convey individual qualities of the model. Portrait of Count Mikhail Vorontsov, a general who participated in the war against Napoleon and a prominent

230 /231 /232

RICHARD PARKES BONINGTON. 1802–1828
BOATS NEAR THE SHORE OF NORMANDY. *Ca* 1825
Oil on canvas. 33.5 x 46 cm

JOSEPH WRIGHT OF DERBY. 1743–1797
AN IRON FORGE VIEWED FROM WITHOUT. 1773
Oil on canvas. 105 x 140 cm

GEORGE MORLAND. 1763–1804
THE APPROACH OF A STORM. 1791
Oil on canvas. 85 x 117 cm

Russian statesman, was painted by Thomas Lawrence in 1821 in London, when Count Vorontsov came with his young wife for a visit to his father, a well-known diplomat, Russia's ambassador to England. The English master represented the count against the stormy sky, lit, as it were, by the romantic halo of a victor and hero. The cloak effectively thrown over one shoulder of the Russian aristocrat, reveals his uniform decorated with the stars of three orders of the Russian Empire: of St Alexander Nevsky, St Vladimir and St George.

Landscape painting began to rise to prominence in English painting towards the end of the eighteenth century. George Moreland was one of the leading masters of this kind of painting. During his short life Morland painted about four thousand paintings, mainly landscapes and genre scenes. He was born into the family of hereditary artists. *The Approach of a Storm* is held to be one of the best landscapes in Morland's huge but not always equally valuable output. Here the artist anticipates the Romantic discoveries of painters at the beginning of the next century — the turbulent, agitated state of nature and man in the presentiment of dramatic ordeals is emphasized by the complex colour scheme saturated with hues and open, dynamic brushtrokes. At the turn of the eighteenth and nineteenth centuries the English school of painting exerted a notable influence on European, especially French art. The early nineteenth century witnessed the flourishing of English art. The work of William Turner and John Constable, who are not represented in the Hermitage, largely determined the development of landscape painting in Europe almost throughout the nineteenth century.

Richard Parkes Bonington, a talented landscape innovator who spent most of his short creative life in France, is represented in the Hermitage by two small canvases. The artist deliberately evaded in his paintings formal classicist views preferring commonplace, ungainly corners He endowed his unassuming motifs with a strikingly convincing mood of calm and poetry, an inimitably individual light and colour effects. The leading representatives of Romanticism, the Barbizon school and Impressionism discovered in the works of this modest English painter the qualities which were exceedingly dear to them. Thus the art of Bonington became a sort of bridge connecting English painting with the best accomplishments of European landscape painting in the nineteenth century.

GERMANY

The Hermitage collection of German art including over seven hundred paintings, about a hundred pieces of sculpture, more than thirty thousand engravings and a great number of works of decorative art is nevertheless inferior to many other collections of the museum as regards its scope. The first paintings by German artists appeared in Russia as early as the reign of Peter the Great, but until the beginning of the twentieth century collectors in Russia as elsewhere in Europe revealed no much interest in the art of this country. There were only two exclusions — Albrecht Dürer and Hans Holbein the Younger — who were often thought to produce works painted by other artists. Thus in 1838 the Hermitage inventories listed eight paintings by Dürer and eight by Holbein, whereas none were in reality produced by them. The Hermitage's paintings of the German Renaissance were mainly eighteenth-century acquisitions — some of them entered the museum with large collections acquired by Catherine the Great — they were rare and were not held to be valuable collectors' items. Seventeenth-century German paintings, which could not rival the creative achievements of Dutch, Flemish, Spanish or Italian artists, were also not in great demand. Works by contemporary German artists, representatives of Neo-Classicism, became popular during the reign of Catherine the Great. The most prominent of them was Anton Raphael Mengs, the founder of the Neo-Classical trend fashionable in the late eighteenth century in Europe, and as a result the Hermitage has amassed a fine collection of works by this master and his contemporaries. The mutual struggle against Napoleon's armies at the beginning of the nineteenth century strengthened Russia's ties with Germany. Many German painters came to work on commissions to Russia. For example, Franz von Krüger, the favourite portraitist of the Russian court, visited St Petersburg six times and created a whole series of formal portraits. Two of his works, the large-scale mounted portrait of the Russian Emperor Alexander I and the likeness of King Friedrich William III of Prussia, adorn the 1812 War Gallery in the Winter Palace. During their tours of European countries, which usually included German cities, members of the royal family visited art exhibitions and artists' studios where they bought a large number of paintings. Nicholas I was a great lover of German art. It is largely to his taste that the Hermitage owes its sizeable collection of German painting and sculpture. As a result almost five hundred years of German painting, from the late fifteenth to the middle of the twentieth century, are represented in the Hermitage. The collection opens with works dating from the age of the Renaissance. The four Hermitage paintings by Lucas Cranach the Elder, a major German master of the first half of the sixteenth century, are good examples of this short but brilliant period in German art. *Venus and Cupid*, *Portrait of a Lady*, and *The Virgin and Child under an Apple Tree* rank among Cranach's masterpieces. They eloquently show the distinctive features of German art in the period when the austere religious spirit of the Reformation harmoniously blended with the ideas of Humanism and national folklore. Cranach's golden-haired Virgin, resembling a princess from an old

THE WINTER PALACE
THE MENGS ROOM

German fairy-tale, is represented amidst a paradise-like landscape. The branches of an apple-tree covered with fruit encircle her head like a luxurious crown. The Virgin's face reflects an ideal of beauty, which is recurrent in most of the artist's works. Cranach's female characters, whether his contemporaries or biblical or mythological images, with a characteristic pure and flowing oval of the face, almond-shaped eyes, golden hair and a gaze bearing some magic secret, are always somewhat mysterious and restrained. A typical example of such a mysterious German beauty is the Hermitage's *Portrait of a Lady*. It is believed that this ideal combined the features of two Cranach's contemporaries revered by the artist — the princess Sybil of Cleve, a well-known beauty at the court of Saxony, and Catharina, wife of Martin Luther, the religious rebel whose friend Cranach was and whose views he shared. The young woman wearing a fine dress, with its numerous details thoroughly delineated by the artist, is represented against a window affording a view of a light, dream-like landscape. A subtle feel for nature was inherent to many German artists — it is not a mere coincidence that Germany, along with the Low Countries, became the birthplace of landscape as an independent kind of painting in the first half of the sixteenth century. *Venus and Cupid* is the earliest of Cranach's numerous works based on mythological subjects. It is generally believed that the Hermitage painting was the first ever attempt in Northern Europe to represent the goddess of love and beauty naked. During the Reformation

233 / 234 / 235

LUCAS CRANACH THE ELDER. 1472–1553
**THE VIRGIN AND CHILD UNDER
AN APPLE TREE**
Oil on canvas, transferred from a panel. 87 x 59 cm

LUCAS CRANACH THE ELDER. 1472–1553
PORTRAIT OF A LADY. 1526
Oil on panel. 88.5 x 58.6 cm

LUCAS CRANACH THE ELDER. 1472–1553
VENUS AND CUPID. 1509
Oil on canvas, transferred from a panel
213 x 102 cm

period the image of Venus was associated in Germany with the dangerous sin of sensuality as is emphasized by the Latin inscription in the upper part of the work.

The German artists of the Renaissance attained particular success in the field of portraiture, a notable example of which in the Hermitage is *Portrait of a Young Man* by Ambrosius Holbein, a talented painter and engraver, who died at the age of twenty-four. Works by Ambrosius Holbein are a great rarity even in German collections. The portrait of a young man was evidently created at Basle, a major centre of Humanism in Germany. It had close ties with Italy and therefore the influence of Italian painting of the High Renaissance in the portrait. However, Holbein's utmost attention to detail in the rendering of human features and his sitter's distinctly German self-concentration and introspection make his work the embodiment of the specifically German national character.

The Hermitage has a large collection of German applied art dating from the sixteenth and seventeenth centuries. It includes silverware produced by Augsburg and Nüremberg craftsmen, fine pieces of porcelain, furniture and jewellery. The Hermitage's collection of eighteenth-century Meissen porcelain is so rich that it is held to be one of the best in the world. The Meissen Factory, established in 1710, earned European renown when it was supervised by Joachim Kändler. His designs were used to produce beautiful vases, grand services, chandeliers and decorative statuettes intended for the embellishment of clocks, mirrors and caskets. Visitors to the Hermitage can see all the basic types of porcelain ware produced at Meissen under the supervision of this master.

The Hermitage collection of nineteenth-century German painting, though relatively small, is considered the best outside Germany. It gives a fairly good idea of the main trends in German art during that period and contains various kinds of painting created by masters from different leading artistic centres of the country. The German collection can be seen in the small second-floor rooms of the Winter Palace, next to the world-famous displays of French art of the turn of the nineteenth

PELLE · CVPIDINEOS · TOTO   CONAMINE · LVXVS
NE · TVA · POSSIDEAT   PECTORA · CECA · VENVS

collection by the Romantic poet Vasily Zhukovsky, who occupied a prominent position at the Russian court as a tutor of the heir to the throne (the future Emperor Alexander II). The Hermitage owes to Zhukovsky a beautiful assemblage of works by the eminent Romantic artist Caspar David Friedrich, which can be rivalled only by the Kunsthalle collection in Hamburg. Zhukovsky, infatuated with Friedrich's art, succeeded in inculcating in Nicholas I, then a grand duke, an interest in the work of this German master. In 1820, on a visit to Dresden, Nicholas attended Friedrich's studio and bought several paintings. He hung them in his summer palace at Peterhof known as the Cottage. The poetic and somewhat melancholic paintings perfectly harmonized with the mock-Gothic architecture of the palace and the landscape park surrounding it.

and early twentieth centuries. Shown there are works by the adherents of the so-called Nazarene school active in Rome and the painters of the Düsseldorf school which came to prominence in the nineteenth century, as well as canvases by the Munich and Berlin painters of the middle and second half of the century.

Many Hermitage paintings from this period came from private St Petersburg collections. The largest of them was the gallery of Count Nikolai Kushelev-Bezborodko. A progressive-minded collector, he bought many works by new European artists, both French and German ones. In 1862, after the owner's death, his gallery was transferred to the Academy of Arts according to his bequest, whence it entered the Hermitage in 1922. Much was done for the enrichment of the Imperial

236 / 237

CABINET WITH A CLOCK. 1700–05
Augsburg. By Johann Valentin Gewehrs
Wood, silver, tortoise-shell, ivory, bronze
Height 96 cm

CLOCK
Meissen. Porcelain, ormolu, painting
over a glaze. 52 x 55 cm

The painting *On a Sailing Ship* was created soon after Friedrich's wedding travel with his young wife to Rugen Island in the north of Germany. Depicted in the foreground of the canvas, the ship moves ahead, seemingly guided not only by the power of wind but by the feelings of the woman and man shown seated at its stern. They are depicted with their backs to the spectator peeping into something visible only to them and personifying the Romantic idea of the beautiful realm created by the artist's imagination. The painting is a poetic dream rather than a reality and it symbolizes the joint sailing of the two lovers across the "sea of life", their mutual aspiration to lofty ideals. After its acquisition by the heir to the Russian crown, the picture was in the private apartments of the future Empress Alexandra Fiodorovna. In 1821 Zhukovsky visited the artist in Dresden again and described in his letter to Alexandra Fiodorovna a new painting by Friedrich which, in Zhukovsky's opinion, would be a fine companion piece to the painting *On a Sailing Ship*. This picture called *Moonrise over the Sea* soon became part of the young princely family's private collection. The canvas is probably the utmost expression of the artist's creative principles. Dominated by a calm and majestic landscape, the canvas contains four figures, all engrossed in a silent contemplation of the sea expanse that merges on the horizon with the endless skies. All the attributes of the Romantic work — the night glistening with a cold moonlight, the silhouette of a sailing ship sliding over the smooth surface, the figures frozen, as it were, in some expectation — serve to evoke a special mood bringing human life in resonance with the life of nature. After a short period of recognition an interest in Friedrich's works almost waned in Germany, probably because "he expressed that what most of people try to evade — solitude". But in the early twentieth century fame has returned to the German artist and nowadays the Hermitage collection of his paintings is one of the most famous in the world.

238 / 239

CASPAR DAVID FRIEDRICH. 1774–1840
MOONRISE OVER THE SEA. 1821
Oil on canvas. 135 x 170 cm

CASPAR DAVID FRIEDRICH. 1774–1840
MORNING IN THE MOUNTAINS
Oil on canvas. 135 x 170 cm

240

CASPAR DAVID FRIEDRICH. 1774–1840
ON A SAILING SHIP. 1818–19
Oil on canvas. 71 x 56 cm

RUSSIA

The Hermitage is traditionally regarded as a museum famous for works of art by Western European and Eastern masters. This is true, but not fully just — the museum has a fairly nice collection of Russian art. Works by Russian artists and craftsmen began to be accumulated in the Winter Palace and the Hermitage in the eighteenth century. Besides, the buildings and halls of the former imperial residence created to designs by outstanding Russian and Western European architects are objects of special pride in their own right. There are more than 330,000 items of Russian culture and art of the sixth to twentieth century including materials yielded by archaeological and ethnographical expeditions, collections of Orthodox icons, works of painting, graphic art, sculpture, decorative and applied art, rare examples of manuscript and early printed books. The Hermitage's displays of Russian art have a specific character since many exhibits are shown in the same palatial interiors for which they were once created or acquired. Works of Christian art occupy a prominent place in the Hermitage's collection of Russian culture. The collection of early Russian icons is of particular interest among them. Although the collection is relatively small, it illustrates fairly well the main Old Russian schools of icon-painting — those of Moscow, Novgorod and Pskov. The icon *St Nicholas*, created in the twelfth – early fourteenth century by an anonymous master of the Novgorod school, ranks with the best examples in the Hermitage collection of Old Russian icons. The saint's face with an open forehead, thinly modelled nose and finely outlined closed lips typifies Christian chastity and immense spiritual power. The deep, austere and kind glance is directed to God — His symbol is the Book

glistening near the heart of St Nicholas. A characteristic feature of the Novgorod school of icon-painting, austere and restrained in style, is the inner tension of an iconic image. The bright red, expressive background of the icon combines with the saturated and succulent tones of the saint's garments in which bluish-green and lemon-yellow tints prevail. The majestic impressions produced by the colourful Novgorod icons of the fourteenth and fifteenth centuries suggests their link with folk art and earlier traditions of mural painting in Novgorod the Great.

According to ecclesiastical notions, the true creator of an icon is God rather than the painter, and so the authors' names are usually absent on icons. This makes the icon *St John the Divine in Silence* particularly interesting. It has an inscription on the reverse reading that the image of St John the Divine was created in 1679 by Nektary Kuliuksin, an icon-painter of the workshop of the Monastery of St Cyril on Lake Beloye, the largest centre of icon-painting in the Russian North. The St Apostle John, Christ's favourite disciple and the author of one of the Gospels, three Epistles and the Apocalypse, is represented in the state of a deep concentration contemplating the Divine Truth. The gesture of the Apostle's right hand touching his mouth is a sign of silence, while the left hand of St John points

THE WINTER PALACE
RUSSIAN CULTURE OF THE SECOND HALF OF THE EIGHTEENTH CENTURY
Part of the display

to the text of the Gospel. Depicted behind the Apostle is the figure of the speaking Angel — the personification of the Holy Spirit and a symbol of the Divine Wisdom.

Moscow craftsmen had long since played the leading role in the production of ecclesiastical objects. The mount of the Gospel datable to 1787–89 is made of silver-gilt. Its upper cover is adorned with enamelled medallions featuring the Evangelists SS John, Matthew, Luke and Mark and a Resurrection scene, as well as two niellated medallions bearing the figures of the Archangels. Truly unique exhibits date from the first quarter of the eighteenth century. This complex of works vividly illustrates the turbulent age of radical transformations in Russia, the birth of the new capital and the activities of the indefatigable reformer Peter the Great. Many items originate from the so-called "Cabinet of Peter the Great" which was scrupulously accumulated in the

241 / 242 / 243

GOSPEL WITH ENAMELLED AND NIELLATED PLAQUE DECORATIONS
1787–89. Moscow. Printing on paper, silver-gilt, glass, chased, engraved, carved and niellated, enamels. 48.5 x 33.5 cm

ICON: *THE LAST JUDGEMENT*
16th century. Kargopol (?)
Tempera on pinewood. 177 x 120 x 4 cm

ICON: *ST JOHN THE THEOLOGIAN IN SILENCE.* 1679
The Monastery of St Cyril of Belozerye
Icon-painter Nektary Kuliuksin
Tempera on panel. 109 x 85 x 3.5 cm

course of decades after the death of the first Russian Emperor and carefully preserved in the Kunstkammer and later in the Winter Palace. The nucleus of the collection is made up of Peter's personal belongings and presents he received on various occasions. One such memorable object is a silver goblet in the form of a one-mast sailing boat, with miniature cannon and figurines of sailors on the deck. Mounted on the prow of the boat is the figurine of a rearing lion with a horn for pouring wine arranged in his mouth. The unusual boat-goblet was produced in 1706 from the first portion of silver gained in the Transbaikal area, as reads an inscription on the stern of the vessel. The famous wax effigy of Peter the Great occupies an honourable place in this group of memorial objects. After the death of Peter I the court sculptor Carlo Bartolomeo Rastrelli was ordered to make exact measurements of the Emperor's body and to reproduce his natural-size figure in wood and wax. The wax effigy, executed by the sculptor within a short

244 / 245 / 246

WAX EFFIGY OF PETER THE GREAT. 1725
Sculptor Carlo Bartolomeo Rastrelli
Height of the figure 204 cm;
armchair 114 x 80 x 58 cm

GRIGORY MUSIKIYSKY. *Ca* 1670 — *ca* 1740
*THE FAMILY PORTRAIT
OF PETER THE GREAT.* 1716–17
Miniature. Painting over enamel
on copper plate. 12 x 8.5 cm

SHIP GOBLET. 1706
Cast, chased and engraved silver-gilt
30.5 x 12 x 37 cm

period of time, possesses an exclusive icono-
graphic value because it gives a faithful notion of Peter the Great's outward appearance.
Nowadays the figure of the monarch is on display in the historical and architectural memorial complex "The Winter Palace of Peter the
Great" which has opened in the basement floor
of the Hermitage Theatre.

No less unique is a collection of Russian enamel
portrait miniatures produced in the first quarter of the eighteenth century. This art enjoyed
Peter the Great's patronage and attained a high
degree of workmanship. The miniatures became items of collectors' interest even during
that early period. The first Russian miniature
painters were active at the Armoury in Moscow where they carried out commissions from
the Emperor and dignitaries in a special workshop producing mainly portraits of Peter and
members of his family. Not infrequently the
miniatures were used as awards given by Peter the Great to his associates. Such portrait
medallions were worn about the neck or in
the tab over the uniform and were prized no
less than the highest state awards. The first
Russian painter who worked in the medium
of enamel miniature was Grigory Musikiysky.
Evidence about his life is unfortunately very
scarce. Originally the talented master was active in Moscow and later at the Armoury Chan-
cellery in St Petersburg. Of especial interest

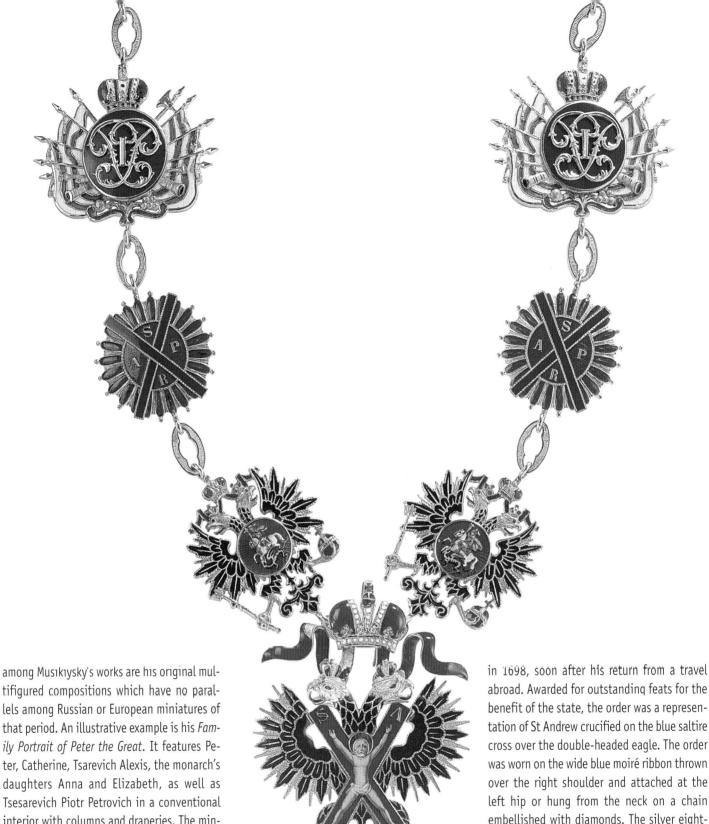

among Musikiysky's works are his original mul-tifigured compositions which have no paral-lels among Russian or European miniatures of that period. An illustrative example is his *Family Portrait of Peter the Great*. It features Peter, Catherine, Tsarevich Alexis, the monarch's daughters Anna and Elizabeth, as well as Tsesarevich Piotr Petrovich in a conventional interior with columns and draperies. The miniature portrait of Catherine I is held to be one of Musikiysky's best works. It shows the Empress wearing a silvery-blue dress with a band of the Order of St Catherine and an ermine mantle, against the luxurious curtain behind which her suburban palace at Ekaterinhof can be discerned.

Peter the Great started the formation of the Russian award system. He instituted the first Order of St Apostle Andrew the First-Called

in 1698, soon after his return from a travel abroad. Awarded for outstanding feats for the benefit of the state, the order was a representation of St Andrew crucified on the blue saltire cross over the double-headed eagle. The order was worn on the wide blue moiré ribbon thrown over the right shoulder and attached at the left hip or hung from the neck on a chain embellished with diamonds. The silver eight-cornered star of the order inscribed with its motto "For Faith and Devotion" was worn on the left side of the breast. On very special occasions the cavaliers put on the special order garments: a green cloak with a representation of St Andrew's star, a white vest and a black hat. The first cavalier of the Order of St Andrew the First-Called was General-Admiral Fiodor Golovin who received this award in 1699. Peter the Great was only the sixth cavalier of the order — he was awarded in 1703. Despite the gradual institution of new decorations, the Order of St Andrew the First-Called still remained the highest award in Russia. The establishment in 1714 of the second Russian award, the Order of St Catherine the Martyr, was connected with the Prut Campaign of 1711 when the Russian army surrounded by the Turkish troops evaded the danger of being destroyed or captured only by a lucky chance.

Tradition has it that Empress Catherine played the main role in the rescue of the Tsar's Army. She received the new Russian award from the Emperor himself. The order was shaped as a cross, original in form, with a depiction of the seated St Catherine on an oval medallion in the centre of it (sometimes shown on a wheel, the instrument of her martyrdom), with a white cross in front of her. Adorned with brilliants or diamonds, the order was worn either on a bow of silk ribbon with the motto "For Love and the Fatherland" on the left side of the breast or on a red ribbon with a silver edge across the right shoulder. The Order of St Catherine was instituted mainly as an award to ladies. The only exclusion was made for the son of the "Most Illustrious" Prince Alexander Menshikov. The Order of St Alexander Nevsky, who glorified himself in the thirteenth century by the victories of his troops over the Swedish and Livonian invaders, was conceived by Peter the Great. It was established, however, only after his death by Empress Catherine I in 1725. The order is a red enamel cross with double-headed eagles between the ends of the cross bearing an equestrian representation of St Alexander Nevsky in its centre. The order was worn at the right hip on a red silk ribbon thrown over the left shoulder. The star of the order depicting the princely monograms encircled by the inscription of the motto "For Labours

247 / 248 / 249

**ORDER OF ST ANDREW
THE FIRST-CALLED ON A CHAIN**
Mid-19th century. St Petersburg
Gold, stamped, cast and chased, enamels
Badge: 6.3 x 8.2 cm; chain: 5.5 x 106 cm

ORDER OF ST ALEXANDER NEVSKY
Late 19th century. St Petersburg
Gold, stamped, chased and engraved, enamels
4.8 x 7.3 cm (with a loop and ring)

ORDER OF ST CATHERINE
Before 1856. St Petersburg
Stamped gold and silver, rose diamonds,
enamels. 5.2 x 8.4 cm

and the Fatherland", was to be worn on the left side of the breast. The Order of St Alexander Nevsky was awarded to members of the higher nobility, both warriors and civilians.

Very popular awards in the middle and second half of the eighteenth century, during the age of "women's rules", were tobacco-boxes made of precious metals and studded with gems and semi-precious stones. The charming boxes, intended for keeping snuff tobacco but quite rarely used for that purpose, were commissioned in large quantities by Elizabeth Petrovna and later by Catherine the Great. The Hermitage possesses one of the largest collections of tobacco-boxes in the world and the bulk of them date from Catherine's reign. Excellent jewellers were active at the imperial court. In the eighteenth century these were mainly foreign master craftsmen who gave a free rein to their imagination not sparing effort or time to meet the demands of their most august commissioners. About 1790 an unknown goldsmith produced a fine golden tobacco-box richly embellished with precious stones and signed it by the letters *P. M. G.* This tobacco-box is sometimes called the "Eastern collection" — under its cover of transparent rock crystal are placed 57 gems, including 28 diamonds, rubies, garnets, spinelles, emeralds, aquamarines and numerous semiprecious stones. All of them serve, as it were, as a luxurious frame for the agate that immediately recalls the cameo with the profile of Catherine the Great. Much more is known about the Swiss jeweller Jérémie Pausier, who lived and worked in St Petersburg for 35 years. He produced for Anna Ioannovna and Elizabeth Petrovna numerous decorations and tobacco-boxes, and for Catherine the Great he created the famous large imperial crown. The "enlightened" and ambitious Empress sought to impart a special grandeur to her reign and she made her court one of the most brilliant in Europe. Outstanding scholars and statesmen, famous generals and poets, talented architects and artists, masters of decorative and applied arts encircled Catherine the Great. Under her patronage the imperial factories manufacturing glassware and porcelain at-tained a European level. They produced exquisite table-services and objects intended for the

decoration of the Winter Palace and suburban residences, decorative vases and small sculpture intended as presents for foreign ambassadors and dignitaries. The Imperial Porcelain Factory was founded by Dmitry Vinogradov, an associate of the famous scholar Mikhail Lomonosov, in the 1740s. During the reign of Catherine the Great the factory not only became a leading enterprise in Russia, but its glory went far beyond the borders of Russia. The age of Catherine the Great saw infatuation with gems and semiprecious stones, which were used for luxurious pieces of jewellery,

250 / 251 / 252 / 253 / 254 / 255

ITEMS FROM THE ST GEORGE SERVICE. 1778
The service designed by G. Kozlov
The F. Gardner Factory
Porcelain, painted in colours over a glaze and gilt

BOUQUET OF FLOWERS MADE OF GEMS AND SEMIPRECIOUS STONES IN GOLD AND SILVER MOUNTS. 1740s. St Petersburg
By Jérémie Pausier. Gold, silver, diamonds, gems, semiprecious stones, glass, fabric. 13 x 19 cm

TOBACCO-BOX WITH A SET OF GEMS. *Ca* 1790
By Master P. M. G. Gold and gems

JOHANN BAPTIST LAMPI THE ELDER. 1751–1830
PORTRAIT OF EMPRESS CATHERINE THE GREAT. 1794
Oil on canvas. 230 x 162 cm

TOBACCO-BOX WITH MONOGRAMS OF CATHERINE THE GREAT AND SEMION ZORICH. *Ca* 1775
St Petersburg. By Jean-Jacques Duc. Gold, silver, brilliants, diamonds, glass, enamels, chased, guilloché and engraved. 3.3 x 7.4 x 5.3 cm (oval)

TOBACCO-BOX. 1740s
St Petersburg. By Jérémie Pausier
Gold, silver, diamonds, sapphires, quartz, chased, polished, poinçon-engraved. 2.6 x 7.4 x 5.3 cm

table decorations, furniture trimming and in the decor of palace interiors. A notable figure among jewellers working for the Russian court in the middle of the eighteenth century was Jérémie Pausier who possessed a perfect skill to juxtapose various gems in new and sudden combinations. The Hermitage owns three bouquets of his work. The bouquet with a tulip made in the 1740s is especially delightful. The luxuriant roses of fiery rubies and garnets are adjacent in it to flowers of cool aquamarines and sapphires. Numerous diamonds playing with hundreds of sparkling hues highlight their pure and noble tones. The tiny flowers, made of corals, white translucent cacholong and tender turquoise enhance the lively charm of the bouquet. The elegant spike of "tiger's eye" aspires to the huge amethyst of the tulip that reigns the entire bouquet. The agate fly hiding on a petal of the red flower to the left imparts a special vivacity to the bouquet.

The traditions of the best Russian and foreign jewellers and stone-cutters of the previous periods were further developed by master craftsmen of the world-famous Fabergé Company. Gustav Fabergé, the founder of the celebrated dynasty of jewellers, passed his business together with his love of classical art to his sons Carl and Agafon. In 1872, on becoming the owner of a private workshop, Carl invited the best goldsmiths of St Petersburg — Erich Colin, August Holmström, Mikhail Perkhin, Henrik Wigström, and Julius Rappoport — to join him. In ten years Fabergé's quick ascent to the peak of fame began. In 1885 Carl Fabergé was granted the title of a purveyor of the Court of His Imperial Majesty. Among the items of jewellery created by the Fabergé Company for the imperial family and the court were famous Easter eggs with all sorts of surprises, as well as brooches, finger-rings, cuff-links, pendants, animal figurines, cigarette- and powder-cases. These articles were used as presents to relatives in the European ruling houses and diplomatic gifts, wedding presents for royal or grand ducal children, presents for the birth of new members of the imperial family, as well as memorial awards to the prominent figures in science and art, officers of the Guard and so on. The family of the last Russian Emperor liked photography and kept the most important pictures in Fabergé frames. A typical example is a silver-gilt frame with red guilloché enamel decoration made at the end of the nineteenth century by Mikhail Perkhin, a leading master of the company. The photograph of Empress Alexandra Fiodorovna with her daughter Tatyana looks

fine between two white semicolumns entwined with delicate shoots, a frieze and a pedestal featuring garlands, bands, rosettes and acanthus leaves. At the Paris World Exhibition in 1900 Carl Fabergé won the Grand-Prix, the Légion d'Honneur, a French order of knighthood, and worldwide recognition. It was Fabergé's

256 / 257 / 258 / 259

CORNFLOWERS WITH SPIKES OF OATS
The Carl Fabergé Company, St Petersburg
Gold, rose diamonds, enamels, rock crystal
Height 19 cm

NARCISSUS
The Carl Fabergé Company, St Petersburg
Cacholong (?), nephrite, rose-cut diamonds, gold, rock crystal. Height 27 cm

**FRAME WITH A PHOTOGRAPH
OF EMPRESS ALEXANDRA FIODOROVNA
AND HER DAUGHTER TATYANA.** Before 1899
The Carl Fabergé Company, St Petersburg
By Mikhail Perkhin. Silver-gilt, two-coloured gold, enamel, ivory; photograph. Height 14.3 cm

**MINIATURE MODEL OF
THE EMPEROR'S REGALIA.** 1899–1900
Hall-marks: the Carl Fabergé Company, goldsmith Julius Rappoport. Gold, silver, platinum, diamonds, spinelle, pearls, sapphires, velvet, rhodonite

miniature (ten times smaller) copy of the Emperor's Regalia that was honoured with the highest award at the Exhibition. The large and small crowns and the orb rest on white velvet pillows supported, in turn, by silver pedestals mounted, like the stand of the sceptre, on the

260 /261 /262

WASSILY KANDINSKY. 1866–1944
WINTER. 1909
Oil on canvas. 70 x 97 cm

WASSILY KANDINSKY. 1866–1944
SKETCH FOR COMPOSITION No 5. 1911
Oil on canvas. 194 x 294 cm

WASSILY KANDINSKY. 1866–1944
VIEW OF MURNAU. 1908
Oil on canvas. 33 x 44 cm

base of a column of pink quartzite. The copy of the large crown is adorned with 1,083 brilliants and 2,458 diamonds, while its smaller counterpart is studded with 64 brilliants and 654 diamonds. After Fabergé was recognized one of the world's best jewellers, his clientele greatly increased. Rich and famous collectors would pay visits to the Moscow branch of the company or to its shops in London, Kiev and Odessa opened earlier, in 1887. Many of them dreamt of acquiring any of Fabergé's elegant "bouquets" in crystal vases — a tender narcissus produced of green nephrite and white cacholong, a twig of sweet peas or deep blue cornflowers adjacent to golden spikes of ripe oats.

Whereas Fabergé and other jewellers of the early twentieth century continued to take their themes from classical art and the natural environment creating in stone and metal an illusion of the real world, painting of this period witnessed different tendencies. Artists tried to express by means of colours their inner world and to explore the abysses of human consciousness. An illustrative example of this innovative trend in Russian art was the work of Wassily Kandinsky, one of the greatest artists of the twentieth century, which is represented in the Hermitage collection by six works. Kandinsky studied at the Academy of Arts in St Petersburg, then he trained in Munich, travelled around Europe and took part in major art exhibitions. Munich, the centre of the German Jugendstil, was Kandinsky's major formative influence. During his stay at Murnau in Upper Bavaria the artist produced his first landscape paintings, in which he began to abandon verisimilitude in favour of conveying his mood by means of pure colour alone. Such is the Hermitage's *View of Murnau* with its dynamic colours and simplified forms. In Kandinsky's landscape *Winter*, painted in 1909, everything shines with the purity of colours: a pink road, a bright yellow house, blue mountains, yellow, green and blue fields. Quests for new means of expression inevitably led Kandinsky to completely discard artistic forms connected with the objective reality. In 1911, in his treatise *The Art of Spiritual Harmony*, the first theoretical foundation of Abstract Art, he asserted that the aim of new art was self-expression rather than imitation of nature. In his series of the so-called *Compositions*, painted between 1909 and 1914, Kandinsky achieved a complete command of colour, which enabled him to produce a picture of an absolute motion, the only beautiful and real thing in the complicated and tragic world of the early twentieth century.

THE HERMITAGE

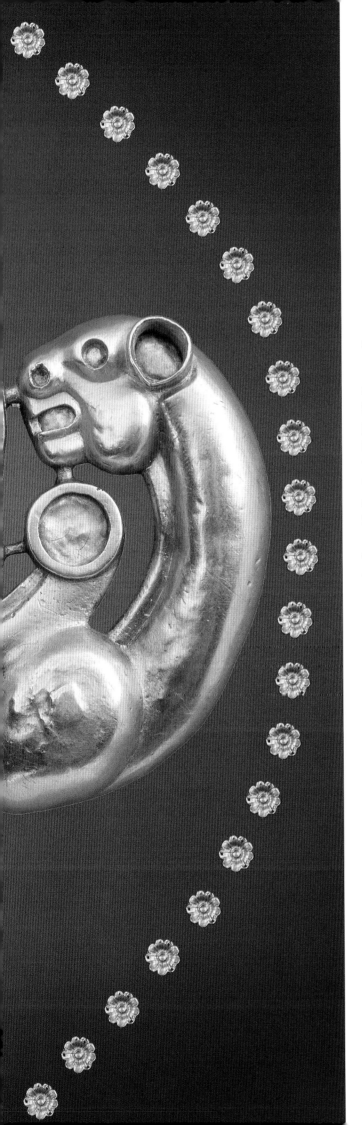

The collection of archaeological relics of the Hermitage representing the ancient cultures of Eastern Europe, Siberia, Central Asia, the Caucasus and Transcaucasia amounts to around 500,000 exhibits. Accumulated on the territory of the former Russian Empire and Soviet Union, it reflects the history of human culture in the course of some three millennia. The first to reveal an interest in hand-made treasures "preserved" by the soil was Peter the Great. In 1718 he issued a decree according to which all unusual finds discovered on the territory of Russia were to be handed over to the state for a corresponding reward and housed in the first Russian museum, the Kunstkammer. Soon a special expedition funded by the state and headed by the German traveller Daniel Gottlieb Messerschmidt went to Siberia. The distant parts, however, attracted the group not by its immense natural riches, but by mysterious golden plaques, full of wild beauty and power. Several examples of them had been brought from Siberia by Nikita Demidov, a prosperous proprietor of foundries as a gift to Empress Catherine I. Peter's reaction was immediate. He ordered the Siberian governor Matvei Gagarin to collect golden articles and send them to St Petersburg. The plaques brought by Demidov were found by "barrow seekers" or adventurers who went to Siberia in search of luck. They quickly understood that the rows of barrows stretching along the rivers Ob and Irtysh were raised over the remains of rich aborigines and conceal immense treasures. Digging out the burials, the "barrow explorers" handed over a part of their gains to the authorities, but most of the discovered golden objects were melted into ingots and sold. Having a large practical experience, these people knew by the outward appearance of the barrows how the burial was arranged and who could have been buried in it. At the turn of the seventeenth and eighteenth centuries burial plundering took a mass scale. Only thanks to Peter the Great's happy interference it became possible to preserve for history 250 golden objects weighing totally about 30 kilogrammes. Later, in the twentieth century, scholars would establish that these objects created between

the seventh century B.C. and first century A.D. belonged to the Saka — the nomadic tribes inhabiting the south of Western Siberia. In 1726 this group of golden articles called the "Siberian Collection of Peter the Great" was handed over to the Kunstkammer to be transferred to the Hermitage in the middle of the nineteenth century. The first half of the eighteenth century was marked by a heightened interest in Siberian secrets. Besides hoard seekers, the area was also visited by scientists, who dreamed of carrying out a scientific exploration of the burial sites. Deserving the greatest merit in this respect was the German scholar Gerard Miller who visited Siberia several times. After Catherine the Great had ascended the throne, the political aspirations of Russia began to be directed southwards. So soon after the annexation of the northern coast of the Black Sea by Russia the direction of archaeological searches also shifted to the south. The late eighteenth and especially the first half of the nineteenth century were marked by sensational discoveries made during the excavations of ancient sites on the northern coastland of the Black Sea. Thus, General Alexei Melgunov, an outstanding statesman of the Catherine age, discovered in the steppes of Southern Ukraine in 1763 a fabulously rich funeral mound of a Scythian chieftain dating from the early sixth century B.C. After the political situation had finally stabilized, the military people were replaced in their explorations by amateur archaeologists — the northern Black Sea coast was literally overwhelmed with seekers of luck and adventure. Admittedly, there were some conscientious researchers among them, too. In 1859 the Imperial Archaeological Commission was established to oversee excavations and to collect the best artifacts for sending them to St Petersburg. By that time professional archaeologists such as Ivan Zabelin, Vladimir Thiesenhausen and Nikolai Veselovsky began to supervise excavations. Under their supervision the work acquired more systematic, scholarly character. By the middle of the nineteenth century a scholarly interest in the distant past of the peoples inhabiting the area of European Russia had markedly grown. This movement was inspired by the archaeologist Alexei Uvarov. In the 1870s and 1880s, in connection with the discovery of a whole world of Palaeolithic art, there appeared enthusiastic researchers, as a rule specialists in natural sciences, who would like to find and explore the sites of primitive people. In the course of the two centuries a long path was traversed from barbarous plundering and destruction of the relics of ancient history to archaeological excavations based on up-to-date scientific methods. After the October Revolution of 1917 a special institute was established at the Academy of Sciences to arrange expeditions to all the distant parts of Russia. Organized on a large scale, this work yielded excellent results. The outstanding archaeologists Mikhail Gerasimov, Mikhail Griaznov, Sergei Rudenko, Mikhail Artamonov, Boris Piotrovsky and many others succeeded in making sensational discoveries on various territories of the vast country. They found palaeolithic sites, rich burials or even whole towns of past civilizations. As a rule, a considerable part of the finds including the best artifacts was given to the Hermitage. Starting from the 1920s, scientists were usually put in charge of the discovered objects of culture and art, and the Hermitage Museum, enriched with a large number of exhibits transferred from nationalized collections, turned into a major centre for the investigation of the primitive world. Its archaeological holdings still continue to be enlarged.

PRIMITIVE ART

A highlight of the Hermitage holdings is the collection of golden articles from the barrow burials of the chieftains of nomadic tribes. This collection of unique objects dating from the seventh century B.C. to the 1st century A.D. is the best in the world. The cattle-breeding tribes roaming over the endless steppe expanses from the Danube to the Amur, had contacts with ancient civilizations and borrowed some elements of alien culture which were acceptable to them. This process found reflection in the development of original art that became known as the "Animal Style" and in turn exerted its influence on the cultural development of the great states. The first nomadic tribes that had left their imprint in the Europeans' memory were the Scythians who came from the depths of Central Asia in the eighth and seventh centuries B.C. and eventually reached the steppes located to the north of the Caucasus. The Hermitage collection of Scythian relics includes numerous examples of weaponry, household objects, horse harness, devotional articles and various items of golden finery. World-famous is the gold plaque in the shape of a stag. Chased presumably in the seventh century B.C., it served as a shield decoration. Admiring the proud beauty of the noble animal, but intentionally distorting its appearance, an unknown craftsman succeeded in endowing the image of the stag with a supernatural might and mysterious sacral meaning. In addition to the stag, the most recurrent and therefore most revered animal image in the Scythian repertory was the panther, a remarkable example of which is a golden plaque found in the Kuban area at the beginning of the twentieth century during the excavations of the Kelermes Barrow. Using the device

of exaggeration characteristic of the Animal Style, the master craftsman makes us feel the beast's cunning, cautious and crafty nature. The tribes of the Saka, a people related to the Scythians, inhabited the south of Western Siberia between the seventh century B.C. and the first century A.D. Their works of art have become known to us thanks to the Siberian Collection of Peter the Great. Represented in this collection are mainly golden decorations — openwork belt buckles and clasps, torques, ear- and finger-rings, bracelets and junctions of horse harness. Most of the buckles, clasps and plaques were cast and then finished with a chisel. The bracelets and torques were made of evenly stretched golden wire and pipes with welded edges. Inlays of coloured paste, corals and semiprecious stones — turquoise, cornelian, etc. — were widely used for decoration. Varied in form and original in their artistic treatment, the articles from the Siberian Collection of Peter the Great testify to the high technical level of Saka jewellers. The massive cast plaque in the shape of a coiling panther is one of the earliest works in this collection. The deliberately extended body and neck of the beast impart to it a sense of both flexibility and fury. One of the nomads' favourite kinds of decoration were torques in the form of a simple neck chain or having a more complex shape. Perhaps the best example in

THE WINTER PALACE
THE KUTUZOV CORRIDOR
Exhibition of the Department of Archaeology

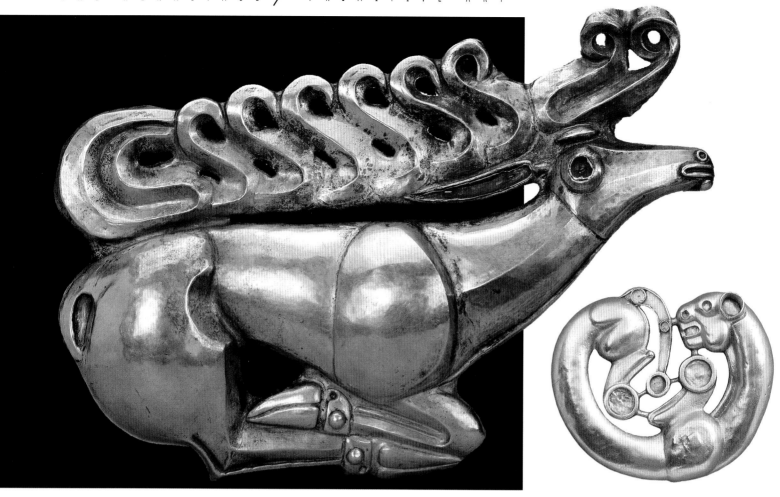

263 / 264 / 265 / 266 / 267

PLAQUE IN THE SHAPE OF STAG
(THE KOSTROMSKAYA STAG)
Late 7th – early 6th century B.C.
Barrow near the Kostromskaya Station,
Northern Caucasus. Gold. Height 31.5 cm,
width 22.5 cm. Weight 634 g

BRACELETS AND NECKLACE. 1st century
Khokhlach Barrow near Novorossiisk,
Rostov Region. Bracelet: gold. Diameter 7.5 cm
Necklace: gold, turquoise, corals, glass
Diameter 17.8 cm, height 6.3 cm

PLAQUE IN THE SHAPE OF COILING PANTHER
7th–6th century B.C.
The Siberian Collection of Peter the Great
Gold. Diameter *ca* 11 cm. Weight 221.2 g

SWORD WITH A RING FINIAL IN A GOLDEN
SHEATH. 7th century
Village of Malaya Pereshchepina near Poltava
(The Pereshchepina Hoard), Ukraine
Gold, iron, glass. Length 94.2 cm

CLASP WITH A HUNTING SCENE IN A FOREST
4th century B.C. The Siberian Collection
of Peter the Great. Gold, turquoise, corals, glass.
Length 19.7 cm. Weight 464.1 g

the Hermitage collection is a golden torque from the so-called Khokhlach Barrow, a first-century burial, found by chance in 1864 during the construction of a water-supply near the city of Novocherkassk in the Northern Caucasus. The torque consists of three rows of tubular elements decorated above and below with a frieze of fighting lions and griffins. The same burial yielded two golden spiral bracelets decorated with figurines of monsters stealthily following one another. The Sarmatian tribes, which were also related to the Scythians, migrated from the East and occupied in the second century B.C. the steppe between the Danube and the Dnieper, whence the Huns drove them out in the fourth century A.D. Sarmatian art continued the traditions of the Animal Style. In the sixth century the Bulgar tribes belonging to the Turkic group of peoples appeared near the Black Sea. The finds of the so-called Pereshchepina Hoard give some idea of their art. A magnificent example coming from this hoard is the sheathed sword lavishly adorned with gold and inlaid with varicoloured glass. At the end of the nineteenth century the Northern Caucasus amazed the world by another sensational discovery — a burial dating from the mid-third millennium B.C. was found on a street at the town of Maikop. The burial contained a log cell with remains of a chieftain and numerous decorations — diadems, rings, beads, golden, silver and bronze vessels. Discovered in the burial were also supports of a canopy, metal rods with the figures of bulls put on them and golden plaques

268

**PLAQUE IN THE SHAPE OF PANTHER
(THE KELERMES PANTHER)**
Second half of the 7th century B.C.
1st Kelermes Barrow, Northern Caucasus
Gold, enamel, garnet. Length 32.6 cm,
width 16.2 cm. Weight 735 g

in the form of pacing bulls and lions which once decorated a fabric. A row of sewn golden rings decorated the lower edge of the canopy.

The most striking and varied complex of archaeological finds in the Hermitage collection is the group of artifacts discovered in the Pazyryk area on the Eastern Altai Territory in the 1930s–1950s. In the fifth and fourth centuries B.C. the tribes of ancient Altaians lived on the plain and in winter migrated to mountains where at the altitude of more than 1500 metres above sea level the graves of their ancestors were located. Water easily infiltrated through

269 / 270 / 271 / 272

FINIAL SHAPED AS A GRIFFIN WITH THE HEAD OF A DEER IN HIS BEAK. 5th century B.C.
2nd Pazyryk Barrow, Altai Territory,
South Siberia

CHARIOT. 5th–4th century B.C.
5th Pazyryk Barrow, Altai Territory,
Southern Siberia
Wood, leather. Height 300 cm

SWAN. 5th–4th century B.C.
5th Pazyryk Barrow, Altai Territory,
Southern Siberia
Felt. Length 29 cm

SADDLE COVER. 5th–4th century B.C.
5th Pazyryk Barrow, Altai Territory,
Southern Siberia. Felt, leather, horse hair
Length 120 cm, width 60 cm

stone embankments into the chieftains' burials in the mountain regions and quickly froze into eternal ice that did not completely melt during a short summer. Such "icebox" perfectly preserved everything in the burial chamber, at the depth of four metres in log cells framed from larch trunks, for centuries. The excavation of the 5th Pazyryk Barrow in the Altai Mountains carried out by the expedition of Sergei Rudenko in 1949 undoubtedly ranks with the most sensational discoveries of the twentieth century. The archaeologists found under a burial mound a cell with five-metre-long coffin carved of a larch trunk. The sarcophagus contained the mummified corpses of the chieftain and his concubine. Outside the coffin were the following objects: a huge rolled up felt carpet, dismantled chariot, corpses of nine horses, with a mask intended for one of them and decorated above by the wooden head of a stag with branchy antlers. The 5th Pazyryk Barrow yielded a woollen carpet that was the earliest ever known example of pile carpet, evidently produced in Asia Minor. Another carpet, huge in size (about thirty square metres), which must have served as a side of the burial tent, was made of felt in the coloured appliqué technique. The large birchwood chariot, about three metres high, intended for a funeral ceremony and made without a single nail, is unique as regards its state of preservation.

THE HERMITAGE

The first collector of objects dating from the age of Classical Antiquity in Russia was Peter the Great who acquired all kinds of ancient objects for Russia's first museum, the Kunstkammer (Museum of Curios) in St Petersburg. It was during that period that the famous statue *Venus of Tauride* arrived in the city. Beginning with Catherine the Great practically each of the Russian Emperors contributed to the formation of the future Hermitage collection of ancient art. During the reign of Catherine the Great were purchased the collections of John Lyde Brown, Director of the English Bank in London; Philippe Egalité, Duke of Orleans; some articles belonged to the engraver Giovanni-Baptista Piranesi. The collection of Count Ivan Shuvalov also yielded some interesting objects. Nicholas I deserves a special mention among royal collectors. It was during his reign that the regular archaeological excavations of ancient sites in the south of Russia began. Numerous rooms and halls in the then built New Hermitage were designed specially to display ancient vases and sculptures. The most significant event in the second half of the nineteenth century was the sale of the immense collection of Marquis Gian Pietro Campana, Director of the Roman Pawn-Shop. The bulk of the collection was divided between France and Russia. The objects which had once belonged to Marquis de Campana rank with the best pieces in the Hermitage holdings. In addition to these collections, the Hermitage acquired works of ancient art from the architect Auguste de Montferrand, the famous archaeologist Heinrich Schliemann, Mikhail Botkin and many other collectors.

After the revolution of 1917 numerous private collections were transferred to the Hermitage as were many works from liquidated museums. Worthy of mention among the latter are the Museum of the Academy of Arts, the Museum attached to the Stieglitz Central School of Industrial Design and the collection of the Russian Archaeological Institute in Constantinople. It is also necessary to say a few words about selfless activities of Russian archaeologists who discovered many outstanding examples of ancient art. The year 1830 when excavations of the Kul-Oba Barrow on the outskirts of Kerch were carried out may be taken as the beginning of ancient archaeology in Russia. The excavation was organized and inspired by Paul Dubrux, a custom officer, who was a pioneer of studying Greek artifacts of the ancient Bosporan Kingdom. The organization of the Imperial Archaeological Commission in 1859 gave a new impetus to the excavations in the south-west of the Russian Empire. The archaeologists Vladimir Thiesenhausen, Alexander Liutsenko and Ivan Zabelin carried out large-scale excavations, primarily of huge barrows in the area to the north of the Black Sea. Fiodor Gross and Vladislav Shkorpil, Directors of the Kerch Museum, investigated huge necropolises in the environs of Kerch. The ruins of ancient town almost did not attract attention of researchers as they did not yield as many fine and valuable objects as burial sites. Only in the twentieth century began the investigation of the ancient settlements of Olbia and Chersonesus. During the Soviet times activities of Hermitage expeditions dealing with various sites of the northern Black Sea coast were continued on a large scale. Of greatest significance among them were digs of Vladimir Belov at Chersonesus, Mark Khudiak and Nonna Grach at Nymphaeum and Liudmila Kopeikina on Berezan Island. As a result of these excavations the collection of the Hermitage Museum was enriched with a considerable number of unique archaeological exhibits. Nowadays, the Hermitage collection of Greek and Roman works of art is one of the largest in the world. Many objects preserved in the museum's Department of Classical Antiquity are unique and are rightly included in all handbooks and large authoritative monographs devoted to ancient art. This collection is a result of prolonged efforts of Russian rulers, private collectors, museum keepers and archaeologists.

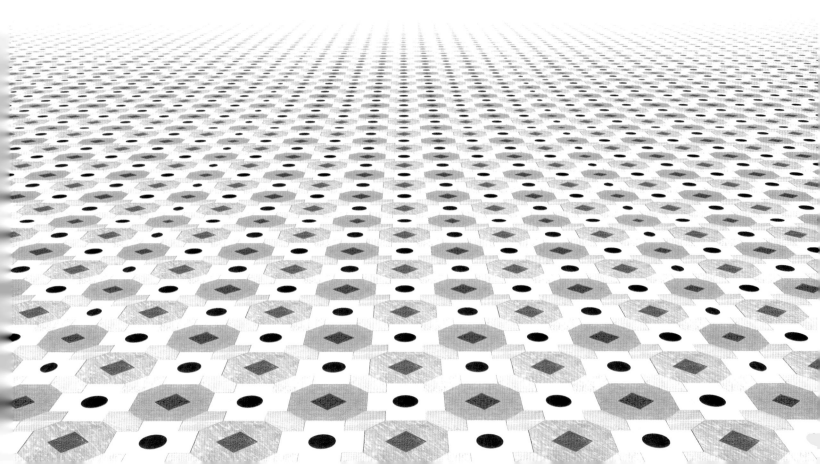

ART OF CLASSICAL ANTIQUITY

The earliest periods of Greek history — the Crete-Mycenaean and Homer ages — are represented in the Hermitage collection by specimens of ceramic vessels and terracotta pieces. Worthy of special attention among them is a fine vase of the twelfth century B.C., the last period of Mycenaean culture. It is adorned with stripes and volutes of brown lacquer, which shows, however, some carelessness characteristic of the period when ancient Mycenae tended to a decline. The Greeks-Dorians brought with them from the north an absolutely new, geometric style of painting, when an ornament in the form of lines, dots, triangles and other geometric figures was applied onto a vessel. The collection includes several goblets, pyxides (ceramic caskets) and a fine cauldron with handles in the shape of goat horns. As early as the third century B.C. the Greeks began to discard the austere geometric style. The acquaintance with the art of Oriental states leads to the emergence of an orientalizing style. It was characterized by numerous depictions of animals, by filling the background with an ornament and by placing depictions in "friezes" or belts encompassing the entire body of a vessel. From the middles of the sixth century B.C. Athens took the leading position in the production of painted pottery. Attic potters worked in black-figure technique, when a silhouette image was arranged on a ground of red fired clay. Additional details were scratched or added with a white red or orange applied colours. For a long time scholars could not reveal the secret of black lacquer used to cover ancient Greek vessels. It turned out that the lacquer was diluted clay applied in a thin coat over the surface and fired in a special way. The Hermitage collection possesses superb examples of black-figure vase painting by such masters as Exekias, Amasis and Lydus. In the second half of the sixth

century B.C. Greek vase painters increasingly turned to the red-figure style. Now all the figures were arranged on a dark background and details delineated with a thin brush. One of the most expressive works of the early (or strict) red-figure style is the famous pelike featuring a swallow, a piece by one of the earliest vase painters working in the red-figure manner. The obverse of the vase bears the record of a conversation of three Greeks — a man, a youth and a boy. The inscriptions indicate what each of them said. "Have a look, this is a swallow!" — says the youth pointing to the bird with his finger. The bearded man raises his head: "Yes, I swear by Hercules!" — "Here it is, spring has come!" — exclaims the boy seated nearby. The reverse of the vessel shows fighting wrestlers. The Hermitage collection includes all kinds of Attic vessels, which are worthy of interest for specialists and lovers of ancient art alike. Especially expressive are figure-shaped vessels. Many of them are made in the form of female heads, like the famous vase of the painter Charin. Starting to apply diverse colours and to decorate vessels with relief details, Greek masters gradually abandoned the red-figure style. The decor of some vases combined old and new devices. Perhaps the most significant example of Greek vase painting dating from the fourth century

THE NEW HERMITAGE
THE JUPITER HALL

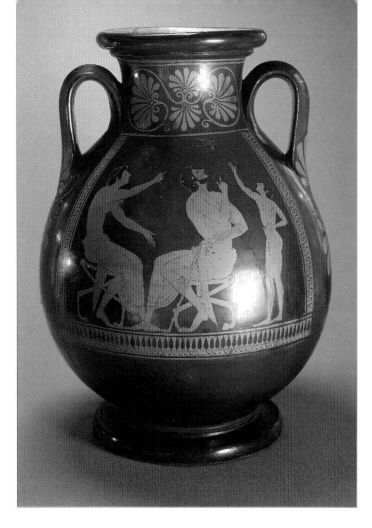

is the hydria that has been known since the nineteenth century under the honourable name of the "Queen of Vases". This hydria was manufactured at Campania, a region of "Great Greece" (as the Greeks named their colonies in the fertile and rich Italy). The black-lacquer surface of the vessel is covered with a sort of flutes imitating a decor of metal vases. The principal adornment of the hydria is a belt of relief images on its shoulders. It portrays the deities of the Eleusine cycle which were worshipped at Eleusis in Attica. Demeter, the goddess of fertility, and her daughter Kore (Persephone) are shown in the centre. Next to them, seated in a chariot harnessed with winged snakes, is Triptolemus,

273 / 274 / 275 / 276

RED-FIGURE PELIKE: *THE FIRST SWALLOW*
2nd half of the 6th century B.C. Attica
Clay. Height 37.5 cm

COMB: *FIGHTING SCYTHIANS.* 4th century B.C.
The Solokha Barrow
Gold. Height 12.3 cm

HYDRIA. THE "QUEEN OF VASES"
ELEUSINE DEITIES. 4th century B.C.
Cumae, Campania
Clay. Height 65.5 cm

LEKANE. 4th B.C.
Attica. The Yus-Oba Barrows
Clay. Diametre 38.2 cm

son of the Eleusine king, who was sent by Demeter to teach people to grow grain. Each of the figures was made with the use of a special mould and painted in different colours which partly paled and crumbled with time. The second tier of reliefs including lions, dogs and griffins is on the body of the vessel.

The largest number of precious objects, which allow us to see how skilful were ancient metalworkers, came from burials in the necropolises of Greek towns and barbarian barrows. They allow us to form an idea of the mastery of Ancient Greek metalworkers. The Scythian leaders made wide use of diverse objects arriving from ancient centres. Highly illustrative in this respect are artifacts found during the excavations of the so-called royal mounds in the steppes near the Dnieper area. A remarkable object created by a Greek jeweller was found during the excavations of the eighteen-metre Solokha Barrow. This is a golden hair comb that was discovered

directly in the royal burial. The upper part of the comb is adorned with five figurines of recumbent lions and right over them is a group of three fighting warriors. One of them, with a Greek helmet on his head, is mounted; a bare-headed Scythian with a rectangular shield assists him. Their enemy, in a Thracian helmet, protects himself with a shield. His horse is dead, which is a sign of his imminent defeat. All the figures are carefully delineated; and even insignificant details of clothes and arms are rendered with care. Probably the comb symbolically represents a struggle for power of three heirs of the Scythian ruler. The largest number of Greek artifacts was found in the barrows located near Greek towns. A rich female burial site near Phanagoria (the Taman Peninsula) yielded two vessels for fragrant oils. One of them is shaped like a sphinx — a winged creature with the body of a lion and the head of a woman. The entire surface of the vessel is painted in colours, which have not lost their brightness over the years. A white face encircled with golden curls has a fine appearance.

The pride of the Hermitage collection is the famous Gonzaga Cameo which features

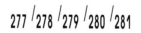

277 / 278 / 279 / 280 / 281

MASK OF RESKUPORIDES (?)
2nd century A.D. (?). Gold. 22.5 x 15 cm

FIGURED VESSEL IN THE SHAPE OF SPHINX. 4th century B.C.
Attica. Phanagoria. Clay. Height 21 cm

STATUE: *APHRODITE ("VENUS OF TAURIDE")*
Roman copy from the original of the
3rd century B.C. Marble. Height 169 cm

THE GONZAGA CAMEO:
PTOLEMY AND ARSINOË. 3rd century B.C.
Sardonyx. 15.7 x 11.8 cm

STATUE: *LUCIUS VERUS.* 2nd century
Rome. Marble. Height 76 cm

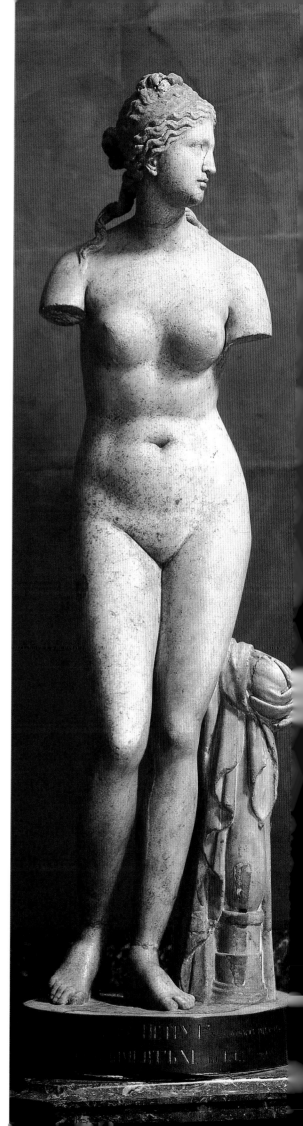

Ptolemy II of Egypt and his wife Arsinoë II. The story of the Gonzaga cameo is full of unusual reversals of fortune. From the collection of the Mantuan dukes it passed to Prague, then the Swedes took it to Stockholm. Christina who resigned the throne and became a Catholic, returned the cameo to Italy. There the carved gem was bought for the Vatican, but later it appeared in France. Eventually, Joséphine de Beauharnais presented the cameo to Alexander I. The hardness of the stone ensured the amazing endurance of the cameo. Set in gold, it looks today precisely as it appeared when the ancient master had finished its carving.

The Hermitage collection of Roman sculpture is quite varied and contains a number of indubitable masterpieces. Roman republican portraits were marked by an utmost realism not infrequently verging on grotesque. An acquaintance with Greek culture led to the emergence of a different trend seeking to idealize the sitter. A struggle between these two trends resulted in such a development of Roman portraiture that it left far behind the achievements of its Greek counterpart. A large demand for park and decorative statuary led to repeated copying of Greek statues. It was in this period that the famous "Venus of Tauride" was created. It is a Roman copy of a Hellenistic statue of Aphrodite. The statue was acquired by Peter the Great in Rome and put on public display on the Neva embankment in St Petersburg. It is natural that the nude Aphrodite shocked the Russian public unaccustomed to such art. As a result, a special guard was put near the sculpture to protect it from "acts of vandalism". Luckily, the wonderful statue lived through all dangers. *Venus* owes its name to the Tauride Palace in St Petersburg in which it had been kept for some time before entering the Hermitage collection. During the Antoninus age it was customary to finish the face carefully leaving the marble surface rough only near the hair. The eye pupil and iris were treated with a particular care. Owing to this portraits of the second century look more spiritual in comparison with their counterparts from earlier periods. A fine example is the portrait of Lucius Aurelius Verus, who shared the imperial powers with Marcus Aurelius. A curious and even somewhat mysterious portrait was found on the territory of the former Bosporan Kingdom that was under a strong Roman influence. The golden funeral mask discovered there was for a long time attributed to the Bosporan king Reskuporides. However, during the recent period even scholars have expressed doubts as to whether we deal here with a male portrait for it seems to have come from a female burial. In any case, the precise delineation of individual features of this mask suggests the influence of Roman art.

THE HERMITAGE

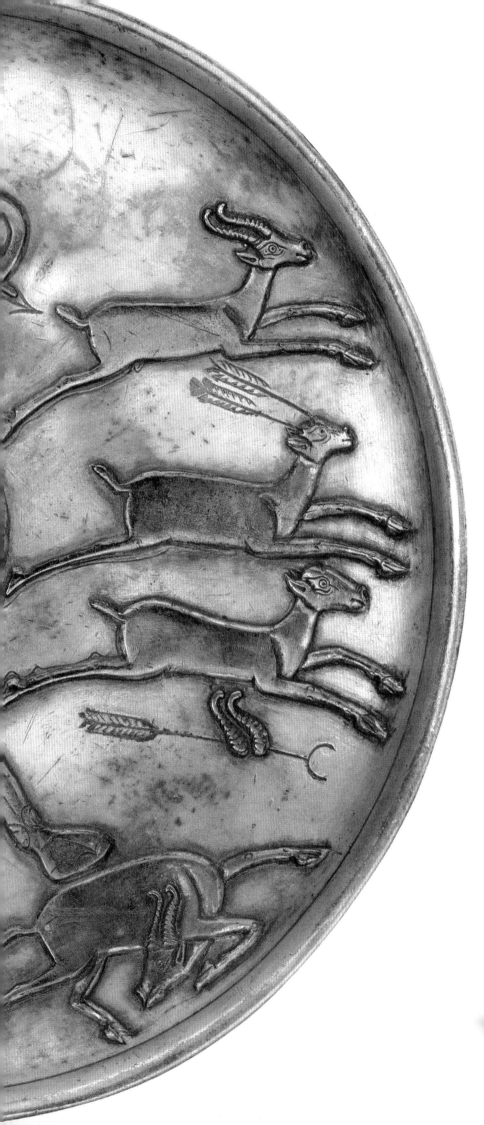

CHINA

The Hermitage collections of relics representing the culture and art of the peoples of the East is large and varied, as is the East itself. There is no unity in these collections — they reflect the age-long paths traversed by different Eastern peoples and civilizations. The collections include both historical cultures which have disappeared and those which have survived to the present-day. The relics of Ancient Egypt, Mesopotamia, Assyria and Palmyra, covering the period from the fourth millennium B.C. to the 4th century A.D., illustrate the most ancient history of this immense region. Works of art from the countries of the Near and Middle East feature the medieval period from the first millennium A.D. to the nineteenth century. The countries of the Far East and South-Eastern Asia, especially China, Japan and Indonesia, are represented by articles ranging from the third millennium B.C. to the second millennium A.D. The formation of the Hermitage's collections of Eastern art began in the reign of Catherine the Great. Her collections were based on luxurious diplomatic gifts of Russia's Eastern neighbours — golden decorations studded with gems, richly ornamented arms and lavishly adorned vases. Originally the treasures of the East were scattered in various repositories of the Hermitage. For example, Catherine the Great's glyptic collection contained,

IRAN

CENTRAL ASIA

along with ancient and Western European pieces, carved gems of Ancient Egypt, Mesopotamia, Persia, Byzantium and China. At the beginning of the nineteenth century, in connection with Napoleon's Egyptian campaign, a vogue for Egyptian objects began to spread in Europe. In 1829 the Academy of Science bought wooden Egyptian sarcophagi which soon came to the Hermitage. In the same period pieces of monumental sculpture also appeared in St Petersburg, notably the statue of the goddess Sekhmet. In the middle of the nineteenth century the first Assyrian objects became the property of the Hermitage, including slabs with reliefs from Nimrud. In 1885 a superb collection of Eastern arms and armour was transferred to the museum from the Arsenal at Tsarskoye Selo. The acquisition of the Alexander Bazilewsky collection yielded fine examples of Byzantine art: diptychs, ivory caskets, mosaic icons and enamels. At the end of the nineteenth century the Hermitage acquired a unique collection of silver from the Sassanian era (3rd–7th centuries) unparalleled anywhere in the world. The rich collection of objects from medieval Persia was enlarged with luxurious carpets and fabrics, lustre ware and masterpieces of Persian miniature painting of the fourteenth to seventeenth century. By 1917 the Hermitage had possessed a large amount of works of Eastern art — about 10,000 items. In 1921 a ceremony of the establishment of the Department of the Medieval or Moslem East, as it was then called, took place. Its first keeper was the gifted young scholar Iosif Orbeli, the future Director of the Hermitage (from 1934). Five years later the department grew into a leading scientific section of the museum, its holdings increased eightfold and it was estimated by specialists as one of the best in the world. In 1933 sensational finds were transferred from the Russian Museum — primarily the unique paintings of the twelfth and thirteenth century found in the "dead" city of Khara-Khoto led by Piotr Kozlov in 1908 and 1909. In 1934 the museum acquired Kozlov's finds from the world-famous Hunnish burials on the territory of Mongolia were also transferred to the Hermitage. In the same 1934 fine relics of Buddhist culture — fragments of wall paintings from cave temples and loess sculpture from the northern oases of Hsinchiang, collected by the expeditions of Sergei Oldenburg in 1909–10 and 1914–15. The collection of Chinese applied art, the largest in Russia, is famous for its masterpieces of stone-carving, traditional red and black lacquers, but primarily examples of celebrated Chinese porcelain. A notable place in the collection of Indian art occupy beautiful Indian miniatures of the fifteenth to eighteenth century, fine fabrics, famous Kashmir shawls, carpets, pottery and weapons. A large number of diverse exhibits came from the regions of Central Asia and the Caucasus. Worthy of particular attention are huge paintings of the seventh and eighth centuries found by archaeologists in Pyanjikent, a medieval Sogdian town located not far from Samarkand. Of especial renown among materials representing the cultures of the Caucasian peoples are relics found on the territory of present-day Armenia, once the area of the ancient state of Urartu. The sensational discoveries, which enabled to carry out a comprehensive study of the culture of Urartu, were undertaken by the Hermitage's expedition led by Academician Boris Piotrovsky between 1949 and 1972.

EASTERN ART

China, the country of ancient traditions with a history of several millennia, occupies a prominent place in the displays of the Department of the East. The culture of China exerted a great influence both on neighbouring countries and distant Europe for centuries. Even the ancient Romans highly prized Chinese silk, and as for Chinese porcelain, its significance for world culture can hardly be overestimated. The Chinese collection of the Hermitage includes ritual bronze vessels, lacquers decorated with carving and painting, masterpieces of stone carving, cloisonné enamels, works of traditional painting, a collection of *nianhua*, or New Year pictures, and, naturally, porcelain. But along with the largest collection of applied art, the Hermitage justly prides itself upon unique finds yielded by Oriental expeditions undertaken at the beginning of the twentieth century.

The early tenth century witnessed the emergence in Central Asia of a semi-nomadic people, the Tanguts. The state Hsi-Hsia created by this people included the Edzina oasis where the city known as Khara-Khoto (the "black" or "dead city" in Mongolian) was established. The Tangut Empire became one of the largest states in Eastern Asia for about 250 years. A wide range of finds from this city — metalwork, pottery, finery and fabrics — confirms this fact. Of special interest are very valuable tapestry-like fabrics, called *keses* or "cut silk". The depiction of Green Tara, one of the most revered female deities of the Buddhist pantheon, executed in this technique, amazes by the skilful execution and variety of blue and greenish tints of silk. The Hermitage owns the best collection of Khara-Khoto paintings datable to the twelfth and early thirteenth centuries. Most of them are religious paintings. Representations of the Shakyamuni Buddha, the Amida Buddha, the most revered of Bodhisattvas (including the compassionate Avalokiteshvara, who refused to become a Buddha in order to help human beings to overcome sufferings) often occur in the paintings. A charac-

teristic feature of the Khara-Khoto paintings is a mixture of such different traditions as the Tibetan and Chinese ones. The Tibetans' depictions of the highest deities are marked by symmetry, austere forms and the brightness of colours filling a clear-cut outline. The mandalas (the word means "circle" in Sanskrit) found at Khara-Khoto go back to the Tibetan trend of Buddhism. The traditional pattern of the mandala, that had become one of the main objects of meditation in Tibet, is usually a combination of concentric circles and squares inscribed one into another and oriented to the cardinal points. This pattern implies the Universe in the centre of which is represented the deity to which this mandala is devoted. Mandalas could be executed in different techniques and materials — woven of pieces of silk or piled up of varicoloured pigments. The collection of Tangut painting includes companion mandalas painted on a wooden support. The only sculptural mandala in Europe devoted to the healing Buddha (Bhaishajyaguru) can be seen in the Hermitage's display of Tibetan culture. The Buddha of Healing was worshipped in Tibet and his depictions occur among the Khara-Khoto paintings. However, in this work carried out according to the Tibetan canon Chinese influences are also present.

THE WINTER PALACE
THE ROOM OF THE CULTURE AND ART OF CENTRAL ASIA

Next to the Buddha are standing the Bodhisattvas of the Sun and Moon with their attributes — correspondingly red and white discs with representations betraying the influence of Chinese pre-Buddhist mythology.

The Chinese artistic tradition, eloquently expressed in a whole number of painted examples, is characterized by a refusal from the strict observance of canons in proportions, colour resolutions and depictions of details, a different imagery, a freer composition and an elegant character of linear design. A typical image is the representation of the Mahasthamaprapta Buddha. The elongated proportions correspond to the vertical form of the scroll. The decorative character of the folds of the clothes, the elegant combination of colour spots with pink and lilac accents make the image unusually ornate demonstrating the influence of Chinese painting of the Sung dynasty.

Chinese potters were the first to evolve porcelain, the secret of which defied discovery in many countries for centuries after them. The Chinese themselves date the development of porcelain in China to the end of the first millennium B.C. European and Russian specialists, however, refer the emergence of definite recipes for the production of porcelain paste to the sixth–seventh centuries A.D. It took whole centuries to find recipes of porcelain paste and glazes, to improve the technology and to create optimal design of kilns for firing the famous Chinese porcelain. For porcelain painting potters frequently used cobalt blue — a rare pigment that stood the heat of the kiln. Alongside traditional underglaze painting in cobalt blue numerous colours for painting over a glaze were evolved with the time. Such pigments demanded much lesser firing temperature, and the development of production enabled to make a second firing to apply colours over the glaze as a painted decor. Chinese porcelain concentrated in itself all those beautiful features that made it an incomparable phenomenon of art. The Hermitage collection contains a wide range of porcelain articles from the fourteenth to eighteenth century. While the diverse articles dating from the fourteenth to sixteenth century show a prevalence of painting in cobalt blue, the wares of the seventeenth and early eighteenth centuries are striking for a wealth of tints in polychrome painted decorations. The characteristic colour combinations of painted decoration dominated by a bright green colour gave name to a whole group of porcelain articles known

as the *Famille Verte*. Articles belonging to the *Famille Rose* are distinguished by the presence in their decoration of an exquisite rose colour the composition of which included colloidal gold. At the end of the seventeenth century so-called "monochrome" wares with their one-colour glaze producing an unusual variety of the subtlest iridescent tints became particularly popular.

The Hermitage boasts the world-best collection of Persian silver of the Sassanian times. Silver and golden bowls, dishes and other vessels were a pride of Persian princes and the nobility. The decor of silverware combined various technical devices: casting with subsequent forging, damascening, chasing, engraving and gilding. As for representations, there was a limited repertory of subjects and a compositional canon both in portraits of the kings and in the depiction

282 / 283 / 284 / 285 / 286 / 287

BHAISHAJYAGURU — THE BUDDHA OF HEALING
Late 12th – early 13th century. Khara-Khoto
Linen (?), mineral colours. 111 x 82 cm

FIGURINES OF LIONS. 18th century
China. Porcelain, painted in enamels

BODHISATTVA MAHASTHAMAPRAPTA
13th century. Khara-Khoto
Silk, mineral colours. 125 x 62.5 cm

DISH WITH PEONIES. Late 17th – early
18th century. China. Porcelain, *Famille Verte*
painted decoration. Diameter 34.5 cm

BOWL ON A LOW RING FOOT
Second half of the 16th century. China
Porcelain, painted in cobalt blue
Height 16 cm, diameter 32.5 cm

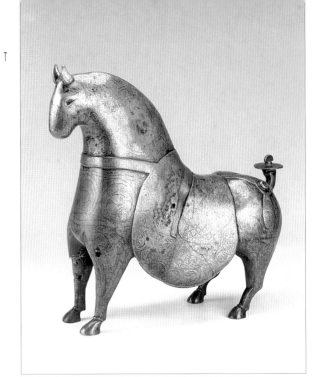

of triumphal battles and victories. The incarnations of the deity of victory (wild boar, horse, bird, lion and Senmurv — a fantastic creature with a dog's body and a bird's wings and paws) appear both as independent representations and in canonic compositions of a "royal hunt". The hunting and feast scenes retained their official significance in Persia and some adjacent regions even after their conquer by the Arabs.

The unification of the Arab tribes inhabiting the Arabian Peninsula in the seventh century beneath the banner of their new religion, Islam, led to a quick conquer of vast territories of Asia and northern Africa and part of Europe. Islam became a state religion in the Arab Caliphate. Early Islamic art preserved many former elements of the past era: bronze figurines of animals and birds produced by Moslem craftsmen had been popular in everyday life of the Sassanian nobility. Islamic craftsmen used composite bronzes shining like gold to produce fine bowls, ewers, candlesticks, incense burners and aquamaniles. A vessel for wine in the shape of an eagle is the earliest exactly dated bronze piece of the Islamic period. It retains an inscription on the necklace decorating a bird and giving the name of the craftsman, Suleiman, and the year of its execution. The expressive rendering of living nature combines with an ornamental pattern covering the entire surface of the bronze. The pattern is interwoven with ornamental Arabic well-wishing inscriptions or quotations from the Koran. The figure of a horse that probably served as a lamp stand is also embellished with an engraved ornament.

True masterpieces in the collection of the culture and art of Central Asia are wall paintings from ancient Sogd. This state, the culture of which developed from the late fourth to the middle of the eighth century, was connected by caravan roads with Persia, India and China. The Sogdians began to establish towns in the northern part of the Silk Road — from Dunhuang to Karashar — thus linking the Orient with the

Near East via Central Asia. These contacts served as a basis for the development of Sogdian art, which is represented by a wide range of fine artifacts — from terracottas and pottery to metalwork and sculpture. But this ingenuous culture found its most remarkable expression in murals coming from ancient temples, palaces and homes of the aristocracy. The decor of a state hall in the palace of the Bokhara oasis ruler at Varakhsha is much different in its colour scheme and artistic effect from other decorative wall paintings. It features several rhythmically arranged groups on an intense red background, among which one recurrent motif is especially notable: a hunter (probably a legendary king), seated on

an elephant, fights against beasts or fantastic creatures attacking him on either side — snow leopards, tigers and griffins. The spots on the snow leopards' skins and the patterns of the clothes enabled the artist to vary the expressiveness and rhythms of the painting. The very appearance of the elephants in murals and some details of the clothes gave rise to the interior's second name — the "Indian Hall". The Sogdian murals, which assimilated the imagery of ancient art of Persia, India and other countries, reveal to us the original world of Central Asian culture.

288 / 289 / 290 / 291

AQUAMANILE IN THE SHAPE OF EAGLE. 796–797
Iraq (?). By Suleiman. Bronze (brass), silver, copper. Height 38 cm

HORSE. Part of a candlestick (?). 10th century
Persia. Bronze (brass), engraved. Height 36 cm, length 42 cm

DISH WITH SHAPUR II HUNTING LIONS. 4th century
Persia. Silver-gilt. Diameter 22.9 cm

SCENES OF SNOW LEOPARD HUNTING. Detail
of wall-painting (the so-called "Red Hall")
7th–8th century. Varakhsha. Sogd

THE HERMITAGE

IVAN FIODOROV ART PUBLISHERS
Russia, 191119, St Petersburg, Zvenigorodskaya ul., 11
Tel./fax: +7 (812) 320-92-01, 320-92-11, 320-92-57. E-mail: info@p-2.ru

Ivan Fiodorov Holding Company is an official partner of the State Hermitage in the field of printing

Ivan Fiodorov Printing Company, St Petersburg (2220)
Printed and bound in Russia